From the Chief of Staff

Following the terrorist attacks of September 11, 2001, the United States and a coalition of like-minded nations embarked on a worldwide campaign against terrorism. In support of this fight, the United States Air Force has played a vital role in Operations NOBLE EAGLE, ENDURING FREEDOM, and most recently, IRAQI FREEDOM. In memory of the victims of terrorism and in consideration of the Airmen who will see this fight through to victory, we must learn and apply the lessons of air and space operations in these joint campaigns. Few causes will ever have greater importance.

One of the most crucial joint combat operations in Afghanistan was Operation ANACONDA, designed and executed to remove the last remaining organized Taliban resistance. Operation ANACONDA generated lessons involving many aspects of the art of joint warfare. These are explored in detail in this report, *Operation ANACONDA, An Airpower Perspective*. This report reminds all Airmen of the complexities inherent in a successful joint operation. It highlights the necessity of clear lines of command, and it reminds us that organizational capabilities and proper coordination of joint activities cannot be taken for granted. It is also vital to realize that lessons learned from this operation were used to improve our joint combat planning and capabilities in Operation IRAQI FREEDOM. As a Service, we will continue to refine the employment of our expeditionary air and space forces in joint operations to ensure their effectiveness over any adversary. We will all benefit from embracing and applying the thorough and thoughtful reporting and analysis in these and other lessons learned reports. We cannot afford to do less.

I thank Dr. Rebecca Grant and the teams of professionals at Task Force Enduring Look and the Office of Air Force Lessons Learned (AF/XOL) who researched and assembled this report. The Secretary of the Air Force and I salute the dedication and sacrifice of all Airmen contributing to our successes in Operations NOBLE EAGLE, ENDURING FREEDOM, IRAQI FREEDOM, and ongoing operations around the world.

JOHN P. JUMPER
General, USAF
Chief of Staff

Published by Books Express Publishing
Copyright © Books Express, 2011
ISBN 978-1-780391-13-7
To purchase copies at discounted prices please contact
info@books-express.com

Table Of Contents

Executive Summary   3

Chapter 1: Introduction   11

    The Roots of Operation ANACONDA   15

Chapter 2: Planning for Operations in the Khowst-Gardez Region

    Early Planning for Khowst-Gardez Area Operations 20
    The Plan Comes Together   24
    Enemy Situation   27
    Estimating Enemy Courses of Action   31
    Hammer and Anvil   32

Chapter 3: Widening the Plan   35

    Planning for Close Air Support   38
    Theater Air Control Prior to Operation ANACONDA 41
    Moving to Bagram and Creating an ASOC Cell   50
    USCENTCOM Approval   55
    Targets for Preliminary Airstrikes   56
    Airlift Requirements   57

Chapter 4: The First 72 Hours: 2-4 March 2002   60

    Pre-Assault Activity   60
    Air Assault by TF *Rakkasan*   62
    Perceptions of Operation ANACONDA after 2 March 2002   66
    3 March 2002   71
    Battle at Takur Gar (Roberts Ridge) 72
    Improving Close Air Support   78
    Assessing the First 72 Hours   80

Chapter 5: Renewing the Attack: 5-15 March 2002   83

    Building Up to Renew the Attack   83
    Valley of Death 85
    Changes in Air Support 88
    Seizing Objective *Ginger* 92
    Afghan Forces Clear the Whale   95

## Chapter 6: Persistent Close Air Support	99

    Hour-by-Hour Airstrike Analysis	104

## Chapter 7: Observations	110

    Some Implications 112
    Training 112
    Planning and Preparation 113
    Execution 116
    Command 118
    Conclusion 119
    Enduring Impact 120

Executive Summary

Operation ANACONDA is a unique case study in the application of force. From 2-16 March 2002, a Combined Joint Task Force (CJTF), built around 1,411 U.S. Army soldiers, and Special Operations Forces (SOF) from the United States and six other nations took on the task of clearing the Shahi Kot valley in eastern Afghanistan of al-Qaeda and Taliban forces who had survived earlier battles. It was a complex, non-linear battle that demanded full integration of Joint forces—and, to the frustration of all, revealed some Joint warfighting stress points.

For the first time in Operation ENDURING FREEDOM, American forces were locked in a prolonged ground battle in difficult terrain. Eight Americans (5 U.S. Army, 2 USAF and 1 U.S. Navy SEAL) died during Operation ANACONDA and 80 were wounded. Seven of those deaths came on 4 March 2002 at the ridgeline at Takur Gar during a helicopter insertion of a Special Forces team and an attempt to rescue them.

Operation ANACONDA also turned out to be an acid test of land and air component cooperation in a pitched fight. The al-Qaeda and Taliban forces holed up in prepared defensive positions in the 10,000-foot mountains and rained mortars and small arms fire down on the Soldiers, Sailors, and Airmen holding blocking positions below. Over the next two weeks, bombers, fighters, helicopters and AC-130 gunships delivered close air support (CAS) into the postage-stamp size battle area measuring about 8 nautical miles (nm) x 8 nm. Deconfliction and coordination of this "fire support" proved challenging with friendly troops and controllers in a small area. In the air, funneling the strikes in was just as intense, and strike aircraft reported several near misses as one pulled up from an attack run while another rolled onto the target. After initial contact sparked heavy fighting, air controllers attached to ground forces or airborne in OA-10 Thunderbolts called in airpower to provide immediate close air support.

Ultimately, Operation ANACONDA was a success. "Operation ANACONDA sought to clear the enemy in that valley area and in those hills," said General Tommy R. Franks, U.S. Army, Commander, U.S. Central Command (USCENTCOM), "and succeeded in doing so where many operations in history had not been able to get that done."[1] However, it was also an object lesson in the complexities of planning and executing rapid air support for ground operations in a hostile, rugged environment.

The report that follows seeks to document air and ground operations during the battle in a case-study format. It offers new statistical analysis from a joint database of the immediate close air support delivered during the battle. Conclusions are left to the reader.

This Executive Summary outlines the principal phases of the battle and the overarching observations from this case study.

Operation ANACONDA developed out of a plan to clear the Khowst-Gardez region of al-Qaeda and Taliban remnants before they could organize a spring offensive and destabilize the interim Afghan government. The fall of Kabul and other cities in November and December 2001 had pushed surviving al-Qaeda and Taliban east toward the high, rugged mountains bordering Pakistan. In early December 2001, a strike at Tora Bora tried to round them up, but many escaped. From 6-14 January 2002, smaller attacks hit Zhawar Kili, site of a well-established al-Qaeda terrorist training camp.

Attention centered on the Khowst-Gardez region because it had a known concentration of al-Qaeda forces and might also harbor top al-Qaeda leaders. Planning for operations in Khowst-Gardez dates back to early January 2002, but the plan didn't come together until early February 2002. Special Operations planners initially met on 6 February 2002, later a small group of the Combined Forces Land Component Commander (CFLCC) planners joined them for another meeting on 9 February 2002. On 17 February 2002, the team briefed their plan to the CFLCC, Lieutenant General Paul T. Mikolashek, U.S. Army, and Major General Franklin L. "Buster" Hagenbeck, U.S. Army, Commander, 10th Mountain Division (Light Infantry) and also CFLCC-Forward (Fwd), who would also command Combined Joint Task Force (CJTF) *Mountain* in this operation.

The Operations Order (OPORD) published 20 February 2002 spelled out CJTF *Mountain's* concept of operations (CONOPS). Working with Afghan forces, the plan was to fight with air assault teams along the eastern ridges. Combat operations would take several hours. CJTF *Mountain's* CONOPS called for "nonlinear simultaneous operations in noncontiguous areas of operations" oriented on the following priority objectives:

(1) Capture/kill al-Qaeda key leaders

(2) Destroy al-Qaeda foreign fighters

(3) Prevent the escape of al-Qaeda foreign fighters

(4) Defeat Taliban forces that continue to resist

The main effort and supporting efforts would effectively box in the area with Afghan forces deployed both west and east of the steep mountain ranges.[2]

But two flaws marred the plan for a swift operation. First, the enemy troop estimates of al-Qaeda and Taliban forces was in dispute with ranges between 168 to over one thousand. Although there were higher estimates by USCENTCOM, the number that made it into CONOPS were much smaller in the Shahi Kot valley itself. After the battle was underway, the CFLCC-Fwd staff calculated the higher end of the spectrum and more than was originally estimated. The gap went unresolved.

The second flaw was that the air component had not been involved in the early development of the plan. Planners all along counted on a certain number of CAS sorties per day based on the estimates of enemy forces in the area. But Lieutenant General T. Michael Moseley, the Combined Forces Air Component Commander (CFACC) did not learn of Operation ANACONDA until 23 February 2002, a mere 5 days before the original start date of 28 February 2002. Neither the land nor the air component had done all they needed to do to put a theater air control system in place to handle close air support requests. Coordination of pre-strike targets, logistics and communications was inadequate.

The final plan for Operation ANACONDA was briefed during a video teleconference with General Franks on 26 February 2002. The CFLCC asked for General Franks to hear comments from General Moseley, who estimated the air component could run "two simultaneous CAS events, given the size of that [area.]"[3]

However, this assumed "deconfliction and orchestration of fires" plus knowing the sustainment requirement, approving pre-planned targets, understanding the rules of engagement inside and outside engagement zones, defining activities for special operations teams, checking the status and equipment of enlisted terminal attack controllers (ETAC) and ground forward air controllers (GFAC) and more.[4] Later that day, 26 February 2002, forecasts of low visibility led to a two-day weather delay.

Operation ANACONDA began on 2 March 2002 as Afghan forces began advancing toward the Shahi Kot valley. Unexpected fire--thought to be from al-Qaeda mortars, but later determined to be accidental fire from an AC-130 gunship--turned back the Afghan force. Still, the air assault went ahead after preliminary sweeps of the landing zones by AH-64 Apache helicopters. But soldiers and special operations forces being delivered by helicopters came under attack almost immediately as they found themselves pinned by fires from hard-core al-Qaeda forces on the mountain slopes above them.

Calls for close air support came fast and furious. The Coalition air component delivered 177 precision bombs (Joint Direct Attack Munition [JDAM] GBU-31s and laser-guided 500-pound GBU-12s) and strafing attacks in the first 24 hours. On the ground, CJTF *Mountain* extracted portions of Task Force (TF) *Rakkasan* from the southern positions—Blocking Points (BP) *Heather* and *Ginger*—and reinforced the northern BPs. Ground forces held on while close air support continued. One SITREP that evening concluded: "Enemy continues to control the high ground in vic [in vicinity of] whaleback [the western ridge of the Shahi Kot Valley] and small fortified pockets throughout the area of operations." The theater reserve was committed to the battle on 3 March 2002. "Numerous bombing strikes were made against dug-in enemy forces vic Babulkeyl resulting in moderate to heavy enemy casualties," the CJTF *Mountain* report noted on 3 March 2002.[5]

Quick reactions by combatants on the ground, persistent close air support, the extraction of forces from BPs *Eve, Heather*, and *Ginger*, and the commitment of the TF *Summit* reserve force contained damage and kept Operation ANACONDA underway. In the first 72 hours, 751 bombs fell into the Operation ANACONDA battle area (495 precision strikes and 256 MK-82s.) For example, bombers delivered strings of 27 MK-82s five times in 15 hours on 3 March 2002. CJTF *Mountain* also noted that the enemy fighters were "staggering from three nights of air strikes."[6]

The tragedy at Takur Gar (later known as Roberts' Ridge) began in the early morning hours of 4 March 2002. Three rocket-propelled grenades (RPG) hit an U.S. Army MH-47 Chinook helicopter attempting to re-insert a U.S. Navy SEAL team.[7] Under intense fire, the MH-47 lifted off rapidly, causing Petty Officer First Class Neil C. Roberts to fall from the aircraft. Then at 0540L, the lead CH-47 from a rescue force was also hit by RPG fire and crashed. Embattled forces fought on the ground all day as F-15Es and other aircraft strafed and bombed al-Qaeda positions only a few hundred feet away.[8]

The task of securing the area and wiping out the concentration of al-Qaeda and Taliban was far from over. CJTF *Mountain* anticipated that "elements already in the Objective *Ginger* AO [area of operation] will continue their movement into preestablished fighting positions to the south and east."[9] A series of airstrikes on al-Qaeda reinforcements helped turn the tide on 5 March 2002. Late in the afternoon, an MQ-1 Predator spotted vehicles and al-Qaeda fighters in a ravine to the south of Objective *Ginger*. Over the next several hours, A-10s, F/A-18s, and an AC-130 gunship attacked al-Qaeda forces. "Target neutralized—200-300 personnel in the open," the ground controller reported.[10] The air support had a direct impact on the battle. "Due to increased bombing and CAS the enemy was unable to sustain any effective fires upon our forces," stated CJTF *Mountain's* evening report on 7 March 2002.[11]

The final phase of Operation ANACONDA consisted of two tasks: taking Objective *Ginger* and clearing a major promontory west of the valley (known as the Whale), so that Afghan military forces could move safely into the Shahi Kot valley. Extensive air support enabled the 9 March 2002 operation to seize Objective *Ginger*. More bombs were dropped from fixed-wing aircraft on 9 March 2002 (327 total) and 10 March 2002 (340 total) than on any other days of Operation ANACONDA. Attack helicopters, fighters, bombers and AC-130 gunships delivered a persistent, lethal barrage for 75 minutes from 1745 local time until 1900. The objective was secured on 10 March 2002.

To clear the Whale and enter the Shahi Kot valley, an additional several hundred Afghan forces moved over "the Whale" on 12 March 2002, while their tanks and additional forces attacked from the north toward Serkhankhel.

Activity in Operation ANACONDA tapered off after 14 March 2002. Two days later, CJTF *Mountain* was able to report to the CFLCC that there were very few enemy personnel in the "entire ANACONDA area."[12] "Thank goodness for the bravery of those soldiers that we were able to take the fight to the enemy and be successful here," said General Richard B. Myers, U.S. Air Force, Chairman of the Joint Chiefs of Staff.[13]

Two major lessons emerged. First was *the critical importance of unity of command*. Throughout this intense operation, no single commander had authority to integrate all the disparate force elements. With the late start in planning, ground and air commanders alike scrambled to correct shortcomings throughout the battle. The second lesson was that *views on the most efficient use and application of airpower differed significantly*. There were gaps in the understanding of tactical procedures for theater air control, and air and ground planners and operators alike were following different doctrinal concepts on the use of airpower in relation to the ground battle.

Operation ANACONDA led both the U.S. Army and the USAF to study shortfalls immediately and correct them. Two sessions of high-level talks on Operation ANACONDA paved the way for better operational linkage between the components. As General Franks said later, "We'll never have the precise picture of any particular place where we're conducting an operation."[14]

"The challenge is to open the aperture on this so that there are more people involved in a process like this, so that the right sets of questions can be asked earlier, and the pre-positioning and the prep tasks can be done prior to execution," noted General Moseley.[15]

And with Operation ANACONDA's sobering lesson in mind, that was exactly what the components did to ensure success in Operation IRAQI FREEDOM a year later.

Chapter One

Introduction

Operation ANACONDA was planned as a brigade-sized operation under the command of 3rd Brigade, 101st Airborne Division (Air Assault), named Task Force Rakkasan and became the biggest ground battle of Operation ENDURING FREEDOM.[16]

Operation ANACONDA began early on 2 March and concluded on 16 March 2002. The CONOPS for Operation ANACONDA was for Coalition forces to attack in the Shahi Kot valley and close off escape routes and trap any fleeing al-Qaeda and Taliban fighters. Instead, both the Afghan and U.S. forces encountered unexpected resistance. The initial *Hammer and Anvil* plan collapsed. All ground forces came under heavy fire from al-Qaeda positions in the surrounding hills and villages. Air controllers, most crammed into a 3 nm x 5.6 nm area, called for close air support (CAS) as the intense battle continued. In the days that followed, the plan was reformulated, troops were reinforced, and air support mechanisms were beefed up. Coalition aircraft delivered an average of more than 250 bombs per day into an 8 nm x 8 nm area about one-sixteenth the size of an Operation DESERT STORM-era killbox. TF *Rakkasan* took their final objectives on 10 March 2002 and Afghan military forces with their embedded SOF teams entered and cleared the Shahi Kot valley a few days later. By 16 March 2002, Operation ANACONDA was over.

For the first time in Operation ENDURING FREEDOM, American forces were locked in a prolonged, bloody ground battle in difficult terrain. Eight Americans died in Operation ANACONDA and 80 were wounded.[17] "Operation ANACONDA sought to clear the enemy in that valley area and in those hills," said General Tommy R. Franks, U.S. Army, Commander, U.S. Central Command (USCENTCOM), "and succeeded in doing so where many operations in history had not been able to get that done."[18] But questions abounded: why was the intelligence estimate off the mark? How had al-Qaeda remnants managed to put up such stiff resistance? Was the ground plan sound? Did close air support provide all it could? Did the mix of SOF forces and conventional forces complicate matters? Had the air and land components cooperated to the best of

air support. Publicity about the operation fueled debate both in the press and in military circles.

While all praised the tactical performance of Soldiers, Sailors, and Airmen alike, there was a pervasive sense that something had gone wrong, and especially that the command and control organizations had all faltered in small ways that added up to significant collective mistakes.

Senior military leaders wanted to learn all they could about the successes and failures of Operation ANACONDA. USCENTCOM produced an after-action report in June 2002, but it was not released. The Air Force began immediate improvements in equipping air controllers and other measures designed to improve close air support. The Army and Air Force Chiefs of Staff led high-level meetings in the fall of 2002 to discuss close air support and other air and land component coordination issues for future operations.

Still, the frustrations and emotions surrounding Operation ANACONDA left a strong impression. As General Franks said of the operation in May 2002:

> The view that we will inevitably get from two or three different people involved in an operation like this will be absolutely factual and valid in the view of the people who are absolutely and honestly on the ground seeing what they saw. And so I would not debate the reports or comments that people have made.[19]

Missing from the debate is an account of what happened on the ground and in the air. This report relies on full sources—reports filed during the operation, immediate after-action reports, statistical analyses, and interviews with participants—to try to fill in a more complete picture of the planning and execution of ground and air operations during Operation ANACONDA.

The remainder of this introductory chapter reviews the roots of the operation. Chapter Two examines the early intelligence assessments of the Khowst-Gardez region, initial planning for the operation and CJTF *Mountain*'s concept of operations as published in February 2002. Chapter Three discusses the air component's effort to put together its plan for airlift and support on a few days' notice and reviews the theater air control system that became so heavily tasked during the battle. The battle itself is divided into two chapters. Chapter Four discusses the first 72 hours, including the deaths of task force personnel at the battle of Takur Gar (afterwards referred to as Roberts Ridge.)

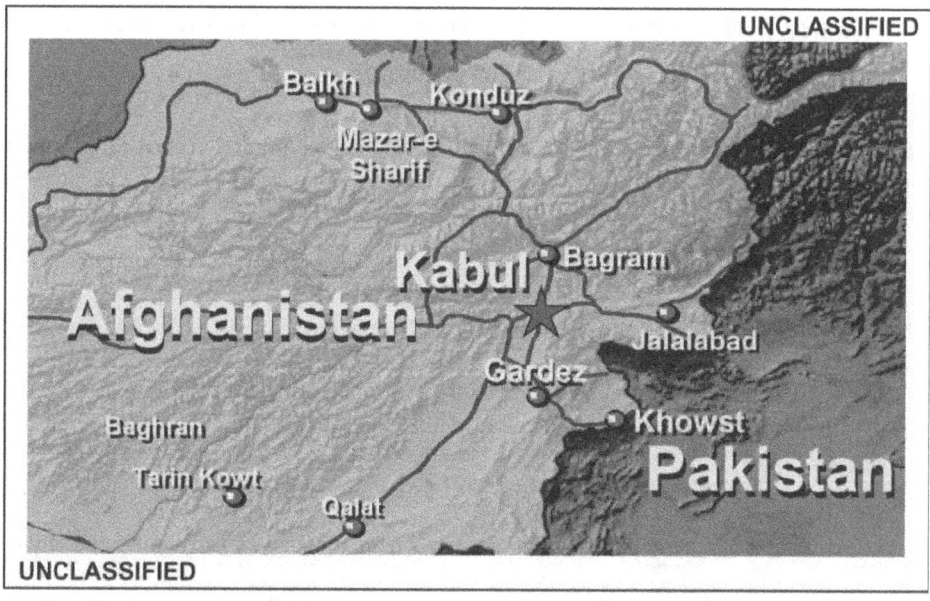

Figure 1: Lines of Communication from Kabul to Gardez[20]

Chapter Five covers task force efforts to renew the attack, the close air support on attempted al-Qaeda reinforcements, and the final seizure of Objective *Ginger* and a terrain feature known as "the Whale." A separate chapter examines statistics of the persistent close air support and its impact on the battle. The last chapter discusses implications and Operation ANACONDA's enduring impact.

The Roots of Operation ANACONDA

Operation ANACONDA appeared to be a unique episode in Operation ENDURING FREEDOM but its roots went back to the battles of November and December 2001. The fall of major cities once controlled by the Taliban forced al-Qaeda and Taliban remnants to retreat to old strongholds. Many al-Qaeda and Taliban managed to flee the battle area in front of Northern Alliance forces.

After Kabul fell on 13 November 2001, one Combined Air Operations Center (CAOC) officer noted that "we sat there with report after report after report of thousands of vehicles leaving Kabul" on the southwestern road leading to the Khowst-Gardez region (see Figure 1). Airstrikes were restricted because of concerns that civilians might be mixed in.[21]

At Konduz, Northern Alliance forces arrived at the outskirts of the town on 20 November 2001. They then permitted a negotiating period to arrange surrenders before they took the town for good on 26 November 2001. As the Northern Alliance gained control of the center of the country, only a limited number of al-Qaeda could make an escape west through Iran. Hard-core al-Qaeda who managed to escape were left with few places to go. Yet many of them—as well as Osama bin Laden and other key leaders—remained at large.

Most of the main hideouts and escape routes lay to the east and south on the semi-circular border with Pakistan. Below the Khyber Pass a switchback indented the border between Pakistan and Afghanistan. Rimming this indentation of the border were some of the region's tallest mountains (see these geographic features in Figure 2).

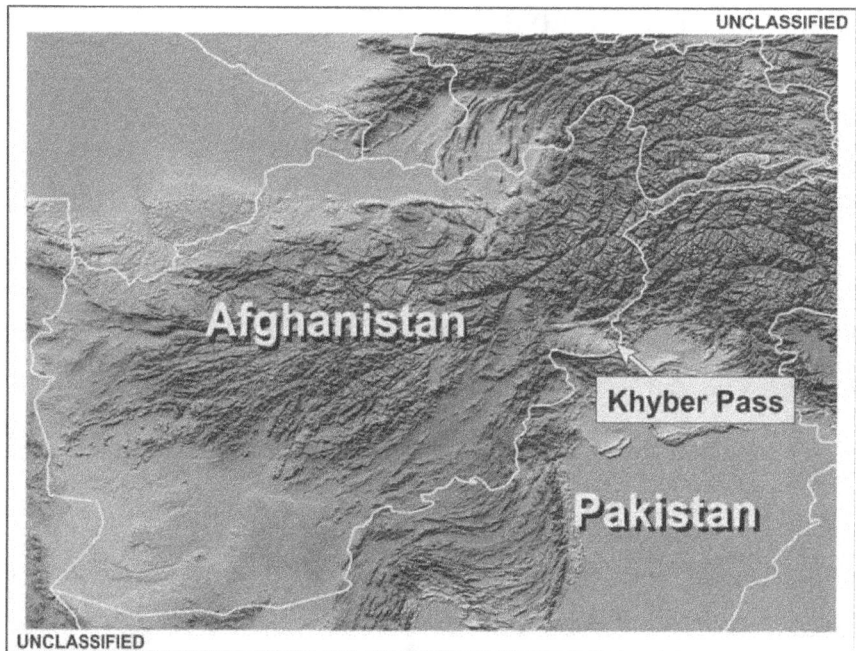

Figure 2: Rugged Terrain of Afghanistan and Pakistan[22]

Chairman of the Joint Chiefs of Staff (CJCS), General Richard B. Myers, described it by noting:

> ...that whole area of Eastern Afghanistan up against Pakistan is very, very rugged territory. The line on the map is just a line on a map...And so you can ebb and flow through that territory as you wish, and you find people that want to support you, and my guess is that bin Laden is moving fairly frequently.[23]

The area General Myers described was home turf for the al-Qaeda. Bin Laden had operated there since the late 1990s and as Taliban control of Afghanistan collapsed the mountains became a refuge again.

USCENTCOM was well aware of the situation. On 9 December 2001, Coalition forces attacked the Tora Bora cave complex. But many Taliban and al-Qaeda escaped again. "There are multiple routes of ingress and egress," noted Vice CJCS, General Peter Pace, U.S. Marine Corps, "so it is certainly conceivable that groups of 2, 3, 15, 20 could [be] walking out of there."[24]

After Tora Bora there was a sense that "because there were not enough boots on the ground, that some bad guys got away. The way to rectify that was to increase the number of conventional forces and turn this into a 'boots on the ground operation,'" commented one officer later involved in air support for Operation ANACONDA.[25]

Secretary of Defense (SECDEF) Donald H. Rumsfeld confirmed on 19 December 2001 that the hunt was still on. "I would think that it would be a mistake to say that the al-Qaeda is finished in Afghanistan at this stage," he said. Some Taliban had "just gone home, dropped their weapons—these are Afghans—and they've gone back to their villages and said, 'To heck with it. I'm not going to do anything.'" On the other hand, the al-Qaeda "do not drift into the villages, particularly," the SECDEF explained. "They're still in pockets. They're still fighting, in some cases."[26]

Coalition forces were also shifting to a different phase of the war. The Combined Forces Land Component Commander (CFLCC) stood up in mid-November 2001 and received tactical control (TACON) of all ground forces operating in theater, including SOF. By the beginning of 2002, Operation ENDURING FREEDOM was trying to move from Phase III "Decisive Operations" to Phase IV, where the emphasis would be on security assistance to the new interim Afghan government.

Before that transition, USCENTCOM still needed to eliminate remaining al-Qaeda and Taliban forces and continue with site exploitation, raiding caves and other caches that might provide information on the Al Qaeda terrorist organization and its future plans. The missions were also trying to confirm or deny the presence of weapons of mass destruction in Afghanistan.

Typical exploitation operations lasted several hours only and rarely encountered enemy forces. This set a pattern of assumptions that would color the planning for Operation ANACONDA.

Chapter Two

Planning for Operations in the Khowst-Gardez Region

Afghanistan in February 2002 was not entirely free of Taliban influence, which posed problems for the Afghan Interim Authority Chairman Hamid Karzai. After Tora Bora and Zhawar Kili, the Khowst-Gardez region appeared to be the center of remaining al-Qaeda and Taliban strength in Afghanistan (see Figure 3). A glance at the map showed why the Khowst-Gardez region was a natural collection point for the Taliban and al-Qaeda forces. The province of Khowst jutted 50 miles eastward into Pakistan like a peninsula. The Khowst-Pakistan border was rural territory—labeled by Pakistan simply as the "federally administered tribal areas." From the city of Khowst, the relatively flat terrain offered easy access to Pakistan. Three major roads led from Khowst to towns inside Pakistan, while river watersheds provided other routes of travel. Refugee camps full of Afghan nationals clustered inside the Pakistan border.

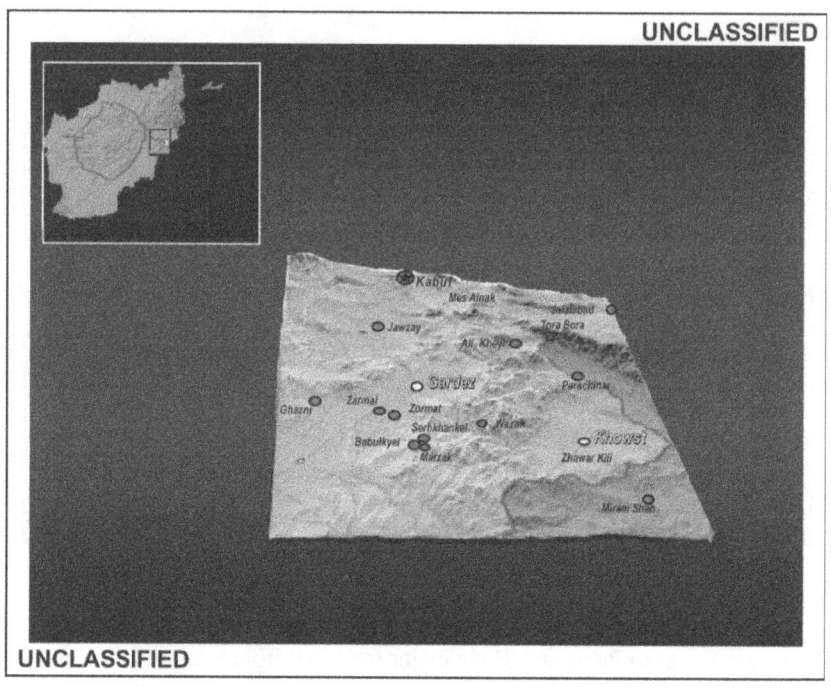

Figure 3: Gardez and Shahi Kot valley[27]

As for Gardez, it was the capital city of Paktia province, with Khowst to the southeast and near the Pakistani border (see Figure 3). All major routes south from Kabul intersected about 75 miles south at Gardez. About 15 miles south of the city, foothills sheltered the Shahi Kot valley, which would be the major focus of Operation ANACONDA.

Early Planning for Khowst-Gardez Area Operations

Preliminary plans for future coalition operations in the Khowst-Gardez region dated back at least to January 2002. On 1 January 2002, a summary titled "CJFLCC Operations" reviewed threats from remaining concentrations of al-Qaeda and Taliban forces in Afghanistan. The threat assessment stated there could significant enemy forces in the region attempting to reconstitute a viable force to counter U.S./Coalition forces entering the area. The objective in the Khowst area was to "clear Khowst-Gardez region of AQ/Taliban elements and pockets of resistance [and] exploit enemy sites."[28] Reports indicated the local populace was sympathetic to the Taliban.

The same January document that mentioned a strong Taliban and al-Qaeda presence in Khowst-Gardez also outlined future military action. It identified the Afghan Commander the "ATF [Afghan Task Force] commander" for operations in Khowst and noted that planning was underway for the objectives in the area for mid January 2002 operations and included raids for high value targets.

The CFLCC published an initial threat assessment and concept of operations for destroying al-Qaeda in Khowst-Gardez and blocking escape routes to Pakistan.[29] The Fragmentary Order (FRAGO) sketched out operations to identify al-Qaeda leaders, foreign fighters, and Taliban members still continuing to resist. The plan called for identifying the al-Qaeda concentrations and working with local Afghan forces. Objectives not suitable for special operations would be singled out for attack by conventional forces. While the original idea was for Afghan forces to carry the brunt of the action, this FRAGO specifically noted that CFLCC would act "in support of Afghan forces when possible. "Critical to success will be synchronizing unconventional and conventional operations to find, positively identify, and destroy enemy forces without collateral damage," the FRAGO stated.[30]

In late January 2002, Combined Forces Commander guidance was issued through the Coalition Target Coordination Board (CTCB). The objectives were:

- Eliminate al-Qaeda pockets of resistance and key Taliban leaders
- Expedite operations IVO [in vicinity of] Khowst-Gardez

- Combine the use of Afghan, coalition conventional, and SF [Special Forces] forces IOT [in order to] systematically sweep and clear Khowst-Gardez
- Focus ISR and solidify IPB [intelligence preparation of the battlefield] IOT facilitate operations
- Operations should be swift (<72 hours) and decisive[31]

The SOF TF was paying close attention to the Khowst-Gardez region as their "next potential target area" according to the Commander of the 20th Air Support Operations Squadron (20ASOS) and the assigned 10th Mountain Division (Light Infantry) ALO, who was at this time working with special operations forces. They "beefed up our numbers of TACPs [tactical air control parties] with these ODAs (operational detachment-alpha) teams" operating in areas like Khowst and Gardez, the Commander stated. By mid-February 2002 there were about six ODA teams operating in the area.[32]

Operation ANACONDA started off as a SOF plan. Initial planning took place during the week of 6 - 13 February 2002. According to this commander, "each one of the task forces had been looking at this area, 70 square miles, for six weeks. The tasker came down for each of the task forces to come up with a plan, how we would handle this concentration, this puddle…of al-Qaeda." Next,

> …The SOF TF came up with a plan, which was not much different than what we had been doing for the previous few months, essentially building engagement zones, special engagement zones in this case, around that area. Cut off various escape routes, run an air campaign against it. Like Tora Bora, bomb the living heck out of it for four or five days, as long as it took, and then slowly tighten the noose on it. We had the advantage here as opposed to Tora Bora… We could put a fishnet around all four sides.[33]

On 6 February 2002, various representatives of special operations forces met in Kabul to establish that "they needed a coordinated battle front." They knew that the Khowst-Gardez area had entrenched al-Qaeda, including Chechen al-Qaeda who would fight to the death. To make it even more tempting, "there was very strong suspicion that this [was] where UBL [Usama (sic) bin Laden] was, because this is where the palace guard was," one SOF participant noted.[34]

On 9 February 2002, the land and special operations component elements met in Kabul. They determined that large concentrations of forces were in the Shahi Kot valley. Reports indicated that enemy forces numbered as high as 1,000 foreign fighters at this point in early February 2002.[35]

However, planners had to make a judgment call about the accuracy of the estimates. Previous experience in Afghanistan showed that sources sometimes overestimated the numbers of enemy forces. In relation to previous engagements, the 20ASOC Commander cautioned: "We used to call it 'Taliban math'" because "the numbers were not worth anything that you could plan around." As a hypothetical example, he explained that a given estimate might be 200-2000 enemy and when the operation was under way, it would turn out to be under 200.[36]

On the other hand, relying on these ground assets was often the only way to gain intelligence. As a later Army report observed:

> The enemy waged primarily a guerilla war in the contemporary operating environment. They did not typically have well-defined organization (order of battle) nor did they employ forces in open terrain. The intelligence required to support this kind of war placed a premium on human intelligence (HUMINT)...[37]

Beginning in early February 2002, the SOF TF began to submit requests for more improved surveillance of the Shahi Kot area. But final planning for new operations had to go ahead without waiting for the final analysis to be resolved.

The Plan Comes Together

The plan for Operation ANACONDA was finalized 10 – 13 February 2002 at the CFLCC-Fwd's new location at Bagram Airfield, approximately 25 nm north of Kabul. Planners from CFLCC/C3, and differing teams worked on operational and collection requirements. Before mid-February 2002, the planning elements that evolved into Operation ANACONDA were "all very conceptual" according to the 20ASOS Commander. It was unclear who would command the operation—10th Mountain, the 101st Airborne, or a SOF commander.[38] While some Airmen, such as the 20ASOS Commander, were involved in preliminary planning since they were embedded with SOF operations, the air component had no role in the planning for Operation ANACONDA at this time.

"Our tasker was to go to Bagram with the SOF TF's operational inputs to the conceptual plans," recalled the commander.[39] Bagram was a combat zone base with limited support and communications available at this time. In fact, the CFLCC-Fwd planning staff was in the midst of moving from support locations to Bagram from 13 – 20 February 2002. The initial planners decided that the complex integration of U.S., Coalition, and Afghan forces demanded a CFLCC-Fwd to assume command of the operation.

The plan now had a name. An individual from the U.S. Army, 5th Special Forces named the concept Operation ANACONDA.[40] But for those not immediately involved in the small-group planning effort, Operation ANACONDA was barely at the rumor stage.

As the plan morphed from a special operations mission to a larger, more complex conventional and special forces operation, the transition time was so brief that the components did not have the chance to initiate, much less complete, a deliberate planning process.

USCENTCOM was becoming strongly committed to mounting operations in this target-rich area for many reasons. CJCS General Myers was briefed on planning for the upcoming operation during his visit to the theater in mid-February 2002. He later said:

> And of course, one of the reasons we want to go in there is not just to eradicate the Taliban and the al Qaeda [sic], but also to gain information, and information that might have impact upon future operations somewhere around this world, and so we'd like some of them to surrender so we can get our hands on them and interrogate them. [41]

Given all these considerations, the ideal operation would be a short-duration seizure of the area with the chance to take prisoners and search the caves and redoubts thoroughly. Planners also assumed that the al-Qaeda might launch a spring offensive around the time of the Islamic New Year on 21 March 2002, and they wanted to wipe out the Khowst-Gardez concentration before then.[42]

The small team led by CFLCC-Fwd representatives had a plan ready to brief by video teleconference (VTC) on 14 February 2002. They then decided to delay the briefing until the CFLCC, Lieutenant General Paul T. Mikolashek, U.S. Army, arrived at Bagram three days later. General Mikolashek, Major General Franklin L. "Buster" Hagenbeck, U.S. Army, Commander of 10th Mountain Division (Light Infantry) and CFLCC-Fwd, and also Commander, CJTF *Mountain*, and all other subordinate task force commanders took the concept brief on 17 February 2002. It appears that the CFLCC was briefed on a concept for a swift operation that would not face heavy enemy resistance. Evidence for this conclusion comes from the CFLCC's reported questions for the briefer. He asked first "what level of understanding does CFACC have regarding this operation at this time?" He then directed "coordination with the CFACC for the estimated number of sorties required for the operation and dedicated airlift support to build the logistics base for the operation."[43] He also asked whether there were not actually too many conventional US forces in the objective area, given the enemy situation estimate. CJTF *Mountain* indicated that civil affairs/humanitarian operations would follow rapidly once areas were secured. The overall tone of this meeting as recorded a few weeks later indicated that there were few major concerns with the concept or with the enemy situation estimate.

On 17 February 2002 at 2100 local time, the CFLCC designated the Afghan military forces as the main effort, took overall command, and ordered the execution date to be no earlier than 25 February 2002, with a target date of 28 February 2002. This gave CJTF *Mountain* barely more than a week to take over an operation that had started out in SOF hands. "I think that's where the ball was dropped first," General Moseley commented later. "I don't think the CFLCC knew what this thing was growing into, and I don't believe the CINC staff knew what this was growing into," he said.[44]

The Operations Order (OPORD) was published on 23 February 2002 and indicated:

> I will use a combination of conventional and special operation forces working in conjunction with Afghan forces (AF) to complete the destruction of identified al Qaeda [sic] leadership, organization, and infrastructure and prevent their escape to Pakistan.[45]

Two main elements were crucial: the assessment of how strong the al-Qaeda and Taliban forces in the area were and what they would do when the attack came.

Enemy Situation

With just days to go before the execution of Operation ANACONDA, a crucial change occurred in the enemy situation estimate. By the time the OPORD was published, CJTF *Mountain*'s official estimate of enemy forces had been telescoped down from a number that took in Khowst-Gardez as a whole to a much lower number pegged only to Objective Remington – the three villages in the immediate Shahi Kot valley. The 126-slide CONOPS briefing put the threat at less than two hundred.

A U.S. Air Force major, who served as the Assistant Division ALO at the Air Support Operations Center (ASOC), understood the lower number came from the CFLCC-Fwd G-2 (or another Army source.)[46] Apparently, CJTF *Mountain* had for some reason narrowed its focus to counting enemy fighters in a smaller geographic area. Instead of tabulating the estimate of enemy forces in the entire vicinity, CJTF *Mountain's* estimate defined the number as those *within* Objective *Remington*.

Already there were indications that the al-Qaeda might put up resistance. For example, Khowst was already a hotspot. The Afghan commander, near the city of Khowst, called for help from airpower during a skirmish on 16 February 2002.

In a taste of what was to come in March 2002, a GFAC directed F-15Es, F/A-18Cs and B-1s to targets, dropping a total of 16 JDAMs. The next day, F-16s dropped JDAMs southeast of Khowst. Even still, forward observers also spotted 35-40 Taliban and al-Qaeda gathering in another location nearby.[47]

Doubts about the numbers generated by various sources now came back to haunt the final planning stages. The late change in the estimate of al-Qaeda and Taliban remnants present in the Shahi Kot Valley area was, in one sense, typical of operations in

Afghanistan, where estimates of enemy strength routinely varied. "It was very similar to the unknown quantities in every other operation," said the 20ASOS Commander.

The difference was that this time, the spread in the estimates might have dictated different tactics or, at the least, larger ground force commitments to achieve better force ratios. Air assault and hammer-and-anvil tactics could sweep up a smaller force of enemy troops. But a larger force of enemy fighters in defensive positions would put up much more resistance, especially when concealed in favorable terrain.

At any rate, the lower number of the OPORD estimate contrasted with other estimates. At the end of February 2002, USCENTCOM produced a different evaluation of the enemy situation that counted Taliban and al-Qaeda independently. USCENTCOM estimated there were "several hundred Taliban fighters" in the area. Many of the Taliban had families in the Shahi Kot valley. USCENTCOM further believed there were an additional several hundred foreign al-Qaeda fighters present. The al-Qaeda fighters did not mix with the villagers but local Afghans fed them. USCENTCOM described the al-Qaeda in Shahi Kot as "dedicated to [the] cause of *Jihad*; eager to fight to the death if confronted."[48] Added together, this made for a total of as many as 1000 Taliban and al-Qaeda in the area.

Strategic reconnaissance pinpointed some "known enemy locations" near Objective *Remington* around 25 February 2002. However, these reports were "skeptically received in the established vetting process" because they did not meet the requirements for "the established deliberate, pre-planned targeting process," a land component report stated later.[49] Further, reports indicated that al-Qaeda and Taliban had paid most of the population of the Shahi Kot valley to leave.

Had a full effort been made to focus ISR assets on the Shahi Kot Valley, the enemy situation estimate might not have been so murky. "We could have set the stage for this much better," General Moseley said. The initial planners did not formulate tailored requirements or contact the air component to do that. Compartmentalization of the planning played a role, too. However, the end result, according to General Moseley, was that there was not a full air and space ISR collection effort tailored to the specific Operation ANACONDA mission prior to the start of the operation.[50]

It was a missed opportunity. The air component had on hand conventional and non-conventional collection assets capable of pinpointing enemy firing positions, routes of travel and personnel in wide area or spot searches. Had General Hagenback's task force requested it, "we could have gone up and just parked over the top of this place and the bad guys would have never known you're there and then just surveyed the whole thing," General Moseley said. "If I had known the plan," he continued, "I could have come back and said to the CFLCC, "give me time to go out and survey this for you and let me go map this for you and I will get all available assets. I mean I'll go out and get you the geologic structure of the OP.'" In fact, General Moseley said he did call General Mikolashek to request guidance on ISR coverage. However, the CFLCC told General Moseley he was waiting for an answer back from General Hagenback at CJTF Mountain on requirements.

For example, the air component already had a track record of providing detailed analysis of sites in Afghanistan. Earlier in Operation ENDURING FREEDOM, Global Hawk was used with an InfraRed sensor to locate men, animals and campfires of al-Qaeda forces around Mazar-e-Sharif and Tora Bora. Although Global Hawk was grounded during the Operation ANACONDA timeframe pending an accident review board, General Moseley commented that if Global Hawk had been available "it would have been sweet." "You could have found one person sitting on one rock and with the support of Global Hawk called in airstrikes "and you could have air-bursted them into the next life."[51]

The enemy forces estimate discrepancy was of particular concern to the CFACC, in part because it might affect air operations. If there were a larger number present, as USCENTCOM claimed, then it stood to reason that the al-Qaeda and Taliban forces might also have crew-served and MANPAD weapons that could threaten aircraft conducting CAS. Hence, the CAOC dealt directly with the USCENTCOM and with the CFLCC to try to resolve it prior to Operation ANACONDA.

General Moseley later said that from his perspective, "We didn't really survey this right, nor did we put the collection assets on this right, nor did we prioritize the collection deck right to find out where these people were, so we would know about where they were and how many there were before we put in our ground teams." [52]

A year later General Hagenback said: "We only probably had about 50% of the intelligence right – locations and more importantly, the enemy's intent, which was to stand and fight."[53]

With no final troop analysis assessment, the larger range of enemy strength estimates dropped off the map. Commanders went forward believing less than 200 al-Qaeda and Taliban fighters would be in the objective area.

Estimating Enemy Courses of Action

Aside from the question of how many al-Qaeda were in the area, the major issue was what they would do when the attack started. As the 20ASOS Commander described the early planning, Operation ANACONDA was different from Tora Bora. At Tora Bora, "we picked out every single cave and came up with several hundred DMPI's (designated mean point of impact) and then decided "to hit every single cave entrance that we can find, as often as required. For Operation ANACONDA: "We knew choke points, so the intent was to get our forces around this piece of land and then gradually work up the LOCs [lines of communications] until we made contact." At any rate, "now we had the 101st in town and the 10th Mountain there to lock those LOCs." The commander thought in mid-February 2002 that once the objective area was encircled, "we were going to kick the hornet's nest with airplanes and then walk up the road carefully."[54]

CJTF *Mountain*'s CONOPS was different. The estimate of the enemy's most probable course of action began with the assumption that al-Qaeda forces and local villagers would receive several hours notice of the beginning of the attack.[55]

Once the operation began, the expectation was that much of the al-Qaeda would flee—by any means possible." The OPORD CONOPS briefing expected the immediate objective would be supporting senior leader security and infiltration. After that, some of the main body would establish defensive positions designed to inflict U.S. casualties or try to take U.S./Coalition prisoners of war. Then, at some point, they would exfiltrate and regroup as conditions permitted.[56]

Ground forces would block off the mountains to the east, pushing the al-Qaeda into the northern or southern escape routes. It was believed that al-Qaeda in the area would defend from caves and mountain BPs [blocking positions] and the primary purpose would be to "divert attention and allow senior leadership to escape." One of the biggest problems would be "sympathetic local leaders" offering bribes to let al-Qaeda forces slip away when the Afghan forces arrived at the villages.[57]

Although analysis indicated that the worst-case scenario would be an organized "defense in depth" of the villages and prepared mountain positions and caves. General Hagenbeck's opinion was that the enemy's objective would still be to let senior leaders escape while inflicting American casualties. "As in Tora Bora, fighters will attempt to exfil [exfiltrate] through severe terrain into ratlines [visible escape routes in the lower Shahi Kot valley] toward Pakistan," the estimate continued. The assessment also assumed that the al-Qaeda would operate in such a way as to avoid drawing air attacks and inviting use of CAS. Likewise, local Taliban remnants might try to move in to attack, but in General Hagenbeck's opinion that would permit massing of troops, making a more lucrative target.[58]

Hammer and Anvil

Having made the case for the al-Qaeda escape behind a light defensive screen, the CTFJ *Mountain*'s CONOP called for "nonlinear simultaneous operations in noncontiguous areas of operations" oriented on the following priority objectives:

(1) Capture/kill al-Qaeda key leaders

(2) Destroy al-Qaeda foreign fighters

(3) Prevent the escape of al-Qaeda foreign fighters into Pakistan, and

(4) Defeat Taliban forces that continue to resist.[59]

According to the plan, the operation was to begin with Special Forces working with the three Afghan military forces. The main tasks were to prepare and position the Afghan forces, and to put special operations teams on the ground to establish a virtual cordon around the Shahi Kot area. Also, a collection of Special Forces began intricate preparations for Operation ANACONDA. Planners demarcated several Areas of Operation (AO) covering the roads and trails east of Khowst on the border with Pakistan.

Then, reconnaissance teams would be inserted and positioned. Next, SOF TF forces would maneuver Afghan forces against enemy concentrations and integrate CAS "as required." Afghan forces moving in from Gardez would be the main effort. To the south, Afghan forces blocked road intersections. On the east side of the mountains, Afghan forces were to set up their blocking positions at the base of the mountains west of Khowst. The main effort and supporting efforts would effectively box in the area with Afghan forces deployed both west and east of the steep mountain ranges.

At the same time, TF *Rakkasan* would conduct the air assault to key positions on the eastern ridges to block escape routes. This would either pin down the al-Qaeda or force them into the hammer and anvil of the Afghan forces. Blocking positions established by regular U.S. and Coalition SOF would stop fighters from crossing the mountains.

All this was to unfold in a very small area. The Shahi Kot valley from the western side of the whale to the eastern ridgeline was about 8 nm x 8 nm. The actual objectives were in an even smaller area. The focus was on three villages, Babulkyel,

Serhkhankel, and Marzak, dotted along the valley floor and thought to contain a significant number of enemy troops. The combat operations phase would terminate when these villages were clear and secure. The combat operations phase was envisioned to last less than one week.[60]

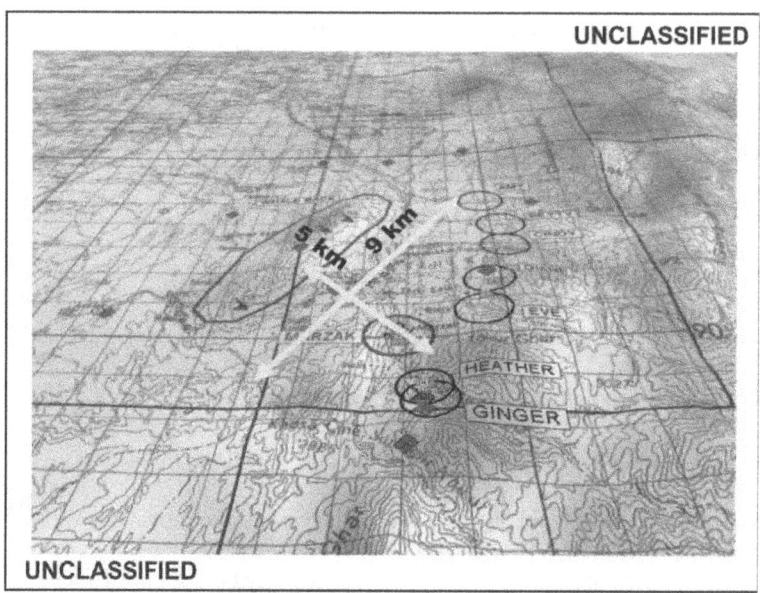

Figure 4: Area of Operations Looking Northwest

The OPORD and related briefings spent very little time on air support and when they did, the main concern was with AC-130 overwatch of key areas and with the role of Apache helicopters and the CH-47s that would be delivering troops.

The OPORD published in February 2002 began as concept that started with SOF operators and was turned into a larger plan by a team that included CFLCC-Fwd and SOF planners. "General Mikolashek and I knew less of ANACONDA than I desired to know at that time," General Moseley commented later.[61] Not much time was left to widen the plan.

Chapter Three

Widening the Plan

The task of coordination with the air component was difficult from the outset—not because there was resistance, but because word of the operation traveled slowly from the CFLCC-Fwd planners at Bagram to the air component headquartered at Prince Sultan Air Base, Saudi Arabia. For example, despite the fact that General Mikolashek directed coordination with the CFACC on 17 February 2002, three days went by before working level coordination began in earnest. Five days passed before any CAOC senior leader got the word.

The total amount of operational-level guidance for the CFACC in the OPORD of 23 February 2002 was contained in six lines of text:

3.C.8. CFACC.

3.C.8.A. Provide CAS for duration of operations.

3.C.8.B. Provide dedicated intra-theater airlift commencing in the early stages to begin building FOB/MSS, through Phase V.

3.C.8.C. Conduct resupply missions to Coalition forces.[62]

Coordination began when the Joint Operations Center (JOC) at Bagram sent their 126-slide ANACONDA CONOPS briefing to the CAOC 20 February 2002. The Battlefield Coordination Detachment (BCD), the CFLCC's liaison element in the CAOC to facilitate operations planning and integration, then used these slides to brief the CAOC/C2 on 21 February 2002. The BCD plunged into planning with the CFACC planners, discussing such topics as a potential carrier gap, when just one carrier battle group would be present, and the need for bombers to cover the firepower shortfall.[63] On 22 February 2002, CFLCC-Fwd sent a detailed message to the BCD plans chief, requesting more assets. First there was good news. According to the staff, CJTF *Mountain* was being briefed that 24-hour coverage was available, but the effectiveness would of course depend on not using up all the on-call airborne ordnance too early in the strike aircraft's vulnerability or *vul* periods. For that reason, there was a desire for more strike aircraft to be made available.

> Looking at the way the ATO [air tasking order] has been built in recent history and as early as yesterday's, we request additional assets for this operation… Unlike the majority of this war, this operation is using an unprecedented amount of conventional, special, and coalition forces. ANACONDA is developing into the first 'real' battle we'll be fighting. Close air support is the primary fire support measure available. Bottom line, we will have a large amount of friendly forces in close proximity to enemy forces….[64]

The message went on to discuss possible bomber surges for lengthier coverage with more weapons and other measures to provide more weapons available for longer periods over the battle area.[65] On 22 February 2002, the CAOC's Master Air Attack Plan (MAAP) team gave the BCD a strawman plan for Operation ANACONDA air coverage.

Although working level coordination was under way, the CAOC Director, Major General John D. W. Corley, U.S. Air Force, first learned of Operation ANACONDA during a routine nightly conference on 22 February 2002. "I was horrified to discover that by the time I had been briefed, the OPORD had already been published without what I thought was the CFACC's knowledge."[66] "I became a little pessimistic about it when the A-heads [senior CAOC staff officers] at the table were not aware of it either," General Corley reported. "That's where I sought to immediately make General Moseley aware so he could engage on it."

General Corley informed General Moseley of the operation; but since General Moseley was traveling, he was not formally briefed on the OPORD until he returned to the CAOC on 25 February 2002.[67] General Moseley later said: "When they came to me with this draft OPORD I said, 'Figure out what it is we need to do to implement or support, and let's get back through CFLCC what it is they're thinking about an overall plan, a detailed plan, and orchestration of effort.'"[68] Generals Moseley and Corley immediately began work on a plan to provide 24/7 bomber coverage and 24/7 fighters armed with "a minimum" of 500-pound laser-guided bombs (LGB).

Elevating the issue had an impact, but time was growing short. By 23 February 2002, the land and air components were hard at work on preparations. CAOC records noted that "Operation ANACONDA was discussed in-depth today." "Teddy R and JFK [two aircraft carrier battle groups] may be swapping out during ops, will step up bombers to cover fighter shortage," the CAOC log stated.

But the number of sorties that could be generated was not the main issue. Air commanders were uncomfortable with the lack of high-level coordination and already apprehensive about close air support arrangements. The problem wasn't supply: there were plenty of U.S. Navy strike aircraft, USAF fighters and bombers available. Coordinating it all would be the issue. General Moseley posed initial questions quoted in the USCENTAF historian's records as: "What are rules of engagement? Will they be relaxed? We need to engage on this now. Twenty-four GFACs will support, so we'll have positive identification (PID)."[69]

During 24–25 February 2002, the CAOC discussed the SOF use of AC-130 gunships during Operation ANACONDA. The main issue was that until 3 March 2002, each night's moon illumination was expected to be high, a risk consideration for the more vulnerable AC-130s. Reconnaissance and surveillance was also a concern so that accurate troop estimates could be realized. On 25 February 2002, the CAOC reported:

> The Taliban and al-Qaeda groups know we're looking for them, and aren't moving. We did first good surveillance last night. Will refine shots now until the 28th. As usual, terrain in the area made taking good shots difficult (deep, narrow valleys). [70]

But the major emerging issue for Operation ANACONDA was close air support.

U.S. Air Force Controller in Operation ANACONDA

Planning for Close Air Support

To employ airborne close air support as the primary supporting fires for the operation, CJTF *Mountain* needed two items: a supply of fighters and bombers over the battle area; and a way to prioritize and deconflict requests that fulfilled CJTF *Mountain*'s intent, while staying in line with the USCENTCOM-imposed rules of engagement (ROE). The first was never a major concern, since as early as 22 February 2002, the

CFLCC-Fwd staff realized they could count on about 60 sorties per day. But the second item, an efficient way to work with the air component to control airstrikes, was left far more to chance and the efforts of a few individuals.

CJTF *Mountain*'s OPORD set up a very small battle area ringed with ground troops that were operating independently but supported with conventional and other assets. While all but one set of these teams were technically under CJTF *Mountain*'s control, the design for Operation ANACONDA made for the most complex airspace control arrangements yet seen in Afghanistan. The battle space was "extremely constrained," General Corley said later. The CAOC would have "B-52s at higher altitudes dropping JDAMs; B-1s at lower altitudes; unmanned vehicles such as Predator flying through there; P-3s, aircraft contributing to the ISR assets; helicopters down at the ground; fast-moving aircraft, F-14s, F/A-18s, F-16s, F-15Es; tanker aircraft that are flying through there. So you begin to see and sense the degree of difficulty of deconfliction," General Corley explained. [71]

On top of all this "we had three civil air routes opened up," added General Moseley. Passengers generated up to three million dollars' worth of revenue a month for Afghan civil carriers. As the CFACC, General Moseley put "bombers above the civil routes, bombers below the civil routes." NGO relief flights used the airspace as did Army helicopters, of which General Moseley said "if they were going to be on the ATO to do strike stuff, we knew what they were doing, but if they weren't, we didn't." [72] Omitted from Generals' Corley and Moseley lists were AC-130 gunships, operating at night under the tactical control of SOF units, providing CAS.

The air control measures that worked earlier in Operation ENDURING FREEDOM were not geared to special forces and conventional forces operating together in a small, congested battle area. "The ROE was not there to go out and do a conventional fight," explained the Director of Combat Operations at the CAOC. Under the rules of engagement for Operation ENDURING FREEDOM, pre-planned strikes, interdiction targets and time-sensitive targets all had to be approved by USCENTCOM; and for the most part, the USCENTCOM/J-2 and legal advisors"... drove what we did and did not target," concluded the Director. GFACs had full authority to call in strikes, but outside Joint Special Operations Areas (JSOAs) that authority only existed if the strikes were *defensive*.[73]

With Operation ANACONDA due to start, nothing had changed. Bombs could still be dropped in only one of three ways: with direct USCENTCOM approval, by opening up an engagement zone or JSOA, or through the defensive reactions of GFACs. Friendly forces would be relying almost entirely on the latter method of GFAC defensive action. That meant that the only *immediate* close air support requests that could be filled under the ROE would come from GFACs who would probably be under fire. Here the hasty transfer of Operation ANACONDA from the SOF world to CJTF *Mountain* caused problems.

CJTF *Mountain*—handed the operation on short notice on 17 February 2002—had never built up the structure needed to process a high volume of CAS requests. As a result "you had a division level headquarters with corps-like responsibilities with a brigade size force," as the Commander, 18th Air Support Operations Group (18ASOG), put it, and no ASOC to prioritize and deconflict.[74] The air component had less than ten days to arrange

40

combat and airlift support for Operation ANACONDA—including two extra days, courtesy of a weather delay.

Theater Air Control Prior to Operation ANACONDA

Here it is necessary to interrupt the chronology of events in the planning for Operation ANACONDA and flash back to Operation ENDURING FREEDOM in the fall of 2001.

Understanding the planning for and execution of Operation ANACONDA first requires a sense of how air support to ground maneuver had deviated—quite successfully—from major theater war doctrine in the fall of 2001, and why the land and air components did not readjust prior to Operation ANACONDA.

Long experience taught soldiers and Airmen that delivering supporting airstrikes in close proximity to ground forces was an intricate process. Army and Air Force doctrine called for setting up an ASOC to deconflict and assign priorities to air support requests from ground forces. A typical ASOC was attached to an Army Corps— a force of roughly three divisions. The CFACC allocated sorties for CAS and pushed them into the airspace; the CAS sorties could then be used by the ASOC to meet Corps tasking.

In a conventional battle, CAS aircraft entering the corps area would first contact the ASOC. Then, the ASOC would "rack and stack fighters and send them out where they need to go, by ourselves, on our radios," explained one of the members of the 18th Air Support Operations Group (ASOG) detached to serve as Fire Support Cell Chief for TF *K-Bar* in the south.[75] The ASOC, with the assistance of the E-8 Joint Surveillance and Target Attack Radar System (JSTARS) performing as an airborne battlefield command

and control center, trained to handle real-time decisions about ground force strike priorities, strike aircraft fuel requirements, remaining time on station, threats in the area, and so on.

But Operation ENDURING FREEDOM had run smoothly without an ASOC so far. No ASOC was required, while no CFLCC existed and while the JSOTF, for all intents and purposes, was the "supported" component commander during operations in October and most of November 2001. Even when the CFLCC stood up, neither ground nor air commanders asked for an ASOC to be established. Rather, air-ground operations continued to be controlled with small Air Control Elements (ACE) imbedded in the various SOF task force Fire Support Cells. The CAOC Chief, Combat Operations later shed light on how, in September 2001, "the ASOC guys came in and said they needed to set up an ASOC."

> Being an ex-FAC, and with my sight picture of how many teams we'd be playing with, I was wondering why we needed to do that…This is a tiny air war. We're looking at perhaps as many as 60-80 strikers a day at any one time. I was like, they can come up on the communications channels because I want to get the SA [situation awareness] of what's happening on the ground level…I thought it was important for us [at the CAOC] to have direct SA, not have an ASOC that's sitting up at CFLCC headquarters in Kuwait that this is getting filtered through. I didn't see where, in this case, it was appropriate to do that. [76]

The CAOC controlled air operations planning and execution by coordinating with its Embedded Special Operations Liaison Element (SOLE) and the individual task force ACEs. The relatively small number of daily strike sorties, the tight procedures for targeting approval and the widely separated battle areas seemed to eliminate the need for formal deconfliction through an ASOC. Not that the battlespace picture was a simple one. As General Moseley said, "in any given space – ground space – out there, you had regular and unconventional forces, humanitarian assistance guys, maybe regular guys and not one of us in the command authority knew where all of those guys were." In fact, the CAOC had the best picture of this crazy quilt because they generally had the locations of all ground forces, conventional forces and to some extent, the friendly Afghan forces. Still, General Moseley commented that he rarely knew where the civilian humanitarian assistance people were, for example.[77] The picture was not complete but the CAOC had the best complete "ground picture" during Operation ENDURING FREEDOM.

The CAOC's daily ATO placed fighters and bombers over the battle area with specific vulnerability periods. A U.S. Navy four-ship of F-14s might have a relatively short vulnerability period of two hours, while a B-1 might be on call for several hours. Support requests from the SOLE were passed on to the E-3 Sentry, the airborne warning and control system (AWACS).[78] The AWACS then directed the orbiting strike aircraft to the targets.

The only requests for airstrikes were from GFACs. The ACEs were manned by a few individuals from Special Tactics Squadrons or experienced Air Support Operations Squadrons (ASOS) and attached directly to the SOF Task Forces. In other cases, SOF qualified enlisted terminal attack controllers (ETACs) were scattered out to act as air controllers. Ground controllers who needed airpower called their ACE. The ACE then called the SOLE at the CAOC at Prince Sultan Air Base. As the U.S. Air Force Commander, 682 ASOS, described it:

> At this point, the two ways to do close air support were either via simplified communications systems to the SOLE. The SOLE would get up and walk across the room and say, "Hey, we have this request." Or people were calling directly to the DDO [defensive duty officer] over secure means. At that point where there were three flights in Afghanistan and four or five teams out at any one point, there was never a real need for prioritization.[79]

The system worked for three reasons. First, the Operation ENDURING FREEDOM battlefield did not require the intricate, formal deconfliction measures needed for true close air support of troops in contact with the enemy. As the 682 ASOS Commander said, "Rather than a linear fight, it was a bunch of guys on lily pads floating around shark-infested waters...."[80] Second, there was more ground-controlled interdiction than true close air support where friendly troops would be even engaged with troops in contact. Controllers' requests often came *in advance* of Northern Alliance troop movements while friendlies were kilometers away from the enemy. Third, the battle areas were geographically separated; controllers working around Mazar-e-Sharif in the north did not have to worry about fellow controllers calling strikes around Kandahar three hundred miles to the south. By the same token, strike aircraft were not likely to bump into each other.

Delivering a fast response to the ground controller was the most important priority. The 18th ASOG Commander said of "part one" of the war:

> The GFAC on the ground literally goes all the way back to the source of airpower to the CAOC, by-passing any kind of natural hierarchy that we build and structure into Army, Air Force, air-land battle. There was no hierarchy at all. That system and part one of the war actually was quite effective because you have a large land mass, a lot of air space, little bitty airplanes with a lot of bombs. Everybody's a bad guy, everything's basically a target. With very small U.S. forces, it's a wonderful way to do it. There are no restrictions to air whatsoever. All of the airspace control measures that you would normally have to worry about in terms of air/ground relationships are not there. All you basically have to worry about is that airplanes don't run into other airplanes. AWACS does a great job of that. None of the battlefield deconfliction was necessary....[81]

The "tiny air war" did not seem to need other measures. Air support grew to depend on a system tailored to a widely distributed ground battle, dominated by special operations forces using air interdiction as fires and Northern Alliance forces as maneuver.

The system worked well in supporting rapid gains by the Northern Alliance, but it had its fragilities. Signs of stress were present well prior to Operation ANACONDA. Two senior field-grade officers who were specialists in air support observed some hiccups. SOF elements essentially competed with each other to have air requests fulfilled, and each learned how to game the system and provide the information that could coax the CAOC into approving its requests. Although the CFLCC was the supported commander in theater after mid-November 2001, CFLCC did not necessarily have much visibility into SOF air requests and how many bombs were being dropped on what targets.[82]

Likewise, the level of experience varied among the task forces on the ground. The Army's 5th Special Operations Group had "some very highly experienced tactical air control parties" and a thorough procedure for briefing the ground teams on special instructions (SPINS) or other changing information. Other units, organized around U.S. Navy SEALs and Coalition forces had GFACs who were less well prepared and who in some cases acted like they "wanted nothing to do with the conventional Air Force."[83] With the exception of TF *K-Bar's* use of conventional air power in the Zhawar Kili area, they had relied almost exclusively on AC-130 gunships to provide CAS.

Then there was the overriding issue: working relationships between the commanders, and particularly the staffs, of the air and land components. The land component was a new player in Afghanistan and as a corporate body, it had not had time to gain experience in how to work with the air component. Tied up in Exercise *Bright Star 01*, mid-September until early-November 2001, the CFLCC and his staff deployed late to Camp Doha, Kuwait, to assume CFLCC duties. This turned out to be a critical shortcoming for Operation ANACONDA.

Much of this was driven by the unique conditions of the war in Afghanistan. By the time the CFLCC stood up on 20 November 2002, the CAOC had been prosecuting a successful war for weeks. However, this was an intricate type of war, with a complicated ROE that set up battlespace control measures that bore little resemblance to conventional doctrine. As General Moseley explained, to strike a target, "you had to either have a JSOA stood up, or a killbox [engagement zone] stood up, or targets outside of that had to be blessed through an elaborate process" reaching "back to Tampa and in some cases back to Washington."[84] The control was so tight that only pieces of the Afghanistan battlespace were "open" for strikes at any one time. Airmen chafed at the restrictions when it caused them to miss opportunities to hit emerging targets, for example. Yet over time, the CAOC grew accustomed to the new style of warfare and adept at handling the intricacies of the coordination process.

The land component did not have the advantage of going through the same learning curve – but until Operation ANACONDA, neither the commanders nor the staffs fully realized that the land component as a whole was not familiar with the USCENTCOM ROE and how it had shaped the character of the war.

In effect, the old doctrinal concepts of control lines and area ownership did not apply. Dozens of JSOAs, engagement zones, special engagement zones, restricted fire areas, no fire areas, off-limits sites of interest, and constant unknowns about friendlies created a jigsaw puzzle of battlespace control measures. It was all very different from the phase lines, corps boundaries and fire support coordination lines of a doctrinally-conventional battlefield. Adding to the confusion, each set of players had their own preferences for handling the control measures for territory where they were operating. Special operations teams on the ground liked to declare whole areas off limits. Army conventional forces were used to owning a defined operating area and being able to call in airstrikes on their own authority. Only the Airmen – who had complained, at least at the working level, about the Afghan theater's restrictions – were routinely familiar with the mosaic.

That meant that the land component and CJTF *Mountain* as its forward node was about to execute operations without grasping how different air and battlespace control would be from usual doctrine. Specifically, the land component did not automatically control all the air-delivered indirect fires on the ground where it was fighting (except for areas beyond a fire support coordination line where aircraft could attack at will.) CJTF *Mountain* did not "own" the territory outside a JSOA or engagement zone. The CFACC owned it – while the combatant commander in Tampa kept authority over certain types of strikes, primarily on leadership targets. This was a new wrinkle. Typically, then, any target not directed as "defensive CAS" by a controller on the ground might well have to be checked with Tampa before aircrews could strike it.

Early phases of Operation ENDURING FREEDOM did not stress the land component enough to point out these weaknesses. Air requests supported the SOF-driven, non-linear battle and the CAOC managed the support requests as part of the bigger picture of strike aircraft, tankers, and airlift working in theater. The CAOC "was acting effectively as an ASOC, because of all the things that were in play," said General Moseley. ASOC personnel in theater were split up to function as ACEs with the various task forces. For example, the CAOC Chief, Combat Operations related how one task force would call controllers to sort out priorities when they had four simultaneous troops-in-contact requests. The CAOC could also deconflict requests, although this process, according to participants, often appeared to depend on "who yelled the loudest."[85]

Gradual changes were in process. For example, more people flowed in to man the CAOC's Battlefield Coordination Detachment beginning in November 2001. Yet the components did not find much opportunity to discuss how they would handle coordination and as a result they did not discover that there were limits on the land component's expertise in how to plan for air support, given the unique rules of the Afghan theater.

Component commanders were in regular contact. However, the working-level relationships did not blossom. According to a later CFLCC report, the CFLCC's daily synchronization video teleconferences (VTCs) that began in November 2001 did not include "formal CFACC representation" until mid-to-late February 2002. BCD, SOLE and Marine Corps liaison officer (MARLO) representatives participated in the VTCs. However, this coordination did not necessarily ensure that word of major impending operations would reach the CFACC or his chief subordinates in time for them to complete full planning.

Not that there were any large-scale operations underway. As 2002 began and Northern Alliance drives on major cities shifted to other target priorities, strike counts plummeted. Bombers and fighters frequently returned to base without dropping any bombs. From mid-January 2002 through the start of Operation ANACONDA the focus was on sporadic requests for support to SOF units, which were usually handled by AC-130 gunships. An ASOC Fires Control Officer explained:

> We built them their airspace control measures, their restricted fire areas, their no-fires areas. We made sure those got into the airspace control order. And then if they needed air, close air support during their missions, we would try to set up as much pre-planned as possible. If they were going to close caves, we'd get them bombers with hard-target penetrating JDAMs. They always wanted gunships, always, always, always. If they needed air during the actual mission, they would always call us at *K-Bar* or K2. We would then coordinate with the SOLE at PSAB. They would get us air by talking to AWACS. [86]

The CAOC and the SOF teams honed their cooperation in Operation ENDURING FREEDOM. Deconfliction was never easy, especially when it came to being absolutely certain where the friendlies were. General Moseley said:

> I think everybody got better at it over time. So you knew how to ask the right questions. You knew how to grab the agency guy and say, 'find out where that team is right now.' [87]

But for CJTF *Mountain*, setting up camp at Bagram just days before the kick-off date for Operation ANACONDA, the Afghan rules were a mystery. The land component had little experience with the deconfliction process or the unusual rules of engagement. The "ROE piece of this was not understood by CJTF *Mountain* at all," General Moseley commented.[88] When CJTF *Mountain* called for air to strike a target, there was a real chance USCENTCOM would still have to approve it anyway. CJTF *Mountain* did not have independent authority to declare targets hostile and could not use airstrikes in the battle area solely as he saw fit.

CJTF *Mountain* was in a whole new ballgame, but this was not well understood. Late February 2002 found the CFLCC Fwd planners getting ready to treat all of the Operation ANACONDA battle area as "short" of the Fire Support Coordination Line (FSCL). They saw "the entire ANACONDA AO as operations short of the FSCL, requiring positive terminal direct control and approval for strike residing with the CFLCC-Fwd Commander."[89] However, as discussed, there was no FSCL and there could be no zone "short of the FSCL" that the CFLCC owned. Here was evidence of the misunderstanding of how to fight in Afghanistan. The ground commander's intent could not override the combatant commanders mandate for all CAS outside JSOAs and engagement zones to be "defensive." High-value targets might also take priority over CAS, and any strike not in a JSOA, an engagement zone, or a trusted ground controller's line of sight might not get hit unless Tampa approved it.

In practice, the limits were even worse than that. No engagement zones were opened up prior to Operation ANACONDA, which eliminated one good method of speeding up air support. A later report suggested that CJTF *Mountain* did not want engagement zones activated.[90] For whatever reason, the delivery of CAS in the battlespace now depended directly and exclusively on the judgment of ground controllers—who, with luck, would have assistance from a small, hastily created ASOC cell.

Moving to Bagram and Creating an ASOC Cell

The move to set up an ASOC cell at Bagram came at the last moment. Senior officers among the air liaison personnel had for several weeks believed they should be planning the stand-up of an ASOC to take place when the Combined/Joint Task Force stood up at Bagram. Key Air Force Colonels collocated with the CFLCC at Camp Doha, began to discuss what they saw as a requirement for an ASOC capability for Afghanistan. They strove to push the air control structure forward.[91] However, neither the CFLCC nor the CFACC formally asked for an ASOC to be set up with CJTF *Mountain*.[92] It was partly a practical issue, as General Moseley pointed out, the CAOC had a high-rate data capacity, which no ASOC would ever have, and the CAOC had been performing ASOC-like functions throughout OEF. But it was mainly an operational issue. Without major land component operations underway, there seemed to be no "demand" for an ASOC.

News of the planning for Operation ANACONDA changed all that. When CFLCC-Fwd, later CJTF *Mountain,* took overall command for Operation ANACONDA on 17 February 2002, the XVIIIth Airborne Corps Commander and U.S. Army Forces Central Command (USARCENT) ALO, 10th Mountain Division's ALO, and his assistant division ALO, and others began to worry about what would happen when 10th Mountain Division got into the fight. The land component was gearing up, too. After the OPORD was released on 20 February 2002, CJTF *Mountain's* Fire Support Coordinator, a U.S. Army Lieutenant Colonel, began to make arrangements for the fire support element (FSE) at CJTF *Mountain*'s headquarters. The Fire Support Coordinator requested the division TACP be sent to Bagram, but did not ask for a full-up ASOC. General Moseley later said, "As this mission shifted to CJTF *Mountain*, somewhere along the way, they missed an opportunity where they didn't have their ASOC and all their gear and communications gear and lash-up with the GFACs."[93]

In fact, 10th Mountain Division had not expected to be tasked with leading an opposed, full-scale conventional assault as they were ultimately assigned to do in Operation ANACONDA. The division deployed to theater in October 2001 with a force protection mission. To keep the footprint small, 10th Mountain Division had to make choices and strip down its forces. For example, the 18ASOG Commander recalled:

> Originally they did not take their TACPs that are normally embedded and lived with them at 10th Mountain. We argued that they made a big mistake. I

personally told General Hagenbeck it was a big mistake. He took more air defense. I said, "Sir, the only people I am aware that you are going to shoot down," I said, will be those aircraft that say "United States Air Force, United States Navy on the tail.[94]

Now, there were just a few days left to make up ground. The 18ASOG Commander dispatched the Assistant Division ALO and three other individuals "and that was the extent of the ASOC experience."[95] They were not yet fully aware of the magnitude of the operation. The Assistant ALO stated, "my thought was, I was going down there to fill the role of the D[ivision]-Main ALO, in the division staff."[96] During a one-day layover at Seeb Air Base, Oman, they agreed to reach beyond that, and try to set up an ASOC cell to support Operation ANACONDA. They arrived in Bagram on 20 February 2002, just as the Operation ANACONDA OPORD was published.

There was not much to work with at Bagram. Over a thousand personnel were living off base operating support (BOS) designed for a smaller complement. U.S. Army soldiers and helicopters were piling into Bagram as a forward staging base. Four Army officers who were West Point professors arrived on the night of February 27, 2002 to assist with planning. "When the sun rose that first morning," one later said, "we were surrounded by bombed out buildings, trash, mines and remnants of Soviet tanks, helicopters, fighter jets and armored personnel carriers."[97] An A-10 pilot later described Bagram as "the scariest place on the planet."[98] Throughout that week, C-17s and C-130s were airlifting fuel into Bagram to support the CFLCC operations and the movement of troops and equipment from Kandahar.

The CFLCC-Fwd's command node was the Joint Operations Center (JOC). The Assistant Division ALO team found that only the 10th Mountain Division staff and the subordinate task force commanders actually intended to work inside the JOC. The 101st

Division liaison officers (LNO) were all...staying at their little headquarters. Obviously that wasn't going to work.[99]

The ASOC cell had no common air picture (much less a ground picture) and needed face-to-face liaison to deconflict and prioritize strikes. The Assistant Division ALO decided to pull them all into the JOC and told the LNOs, "You've got to sit in here because I am going to stand there, and I am going to scream these coordinates out, and you're going to look me in the face and say, 'I've got nobody standing on that spot, so you're clear to strike.'" With that incentive, "they started to migrate in over a few days," He added that although with the operation now just a few days away, it was "very difficult to break into the Army's process of their battle rhythm." "We were a bother to them," he added.[100]

The ASOC cell did conduct several rehearsals for clearance of fires. But they barely had time to get the cell functional. Communications support depended on email, non-secure telephone, and chat systems to get more help from outside. Under its typical operational configuration, an ASOC had lots of equipment and capability, including robust communications, useful data links, and battle management software and displays. This ASOC cell, however, did not have the Common Operating Picture capability, because of inadequate secure communications. CFLCC-Fwd had a JSTARS ground station during early OEF, but did not set up the capability in Bagram.[101] The Assistant Division ALO was not at first able to set up an Air Force air request net (AFARN) and, with 382ASOS backing, he elected instead to rely on the other means.

However, the ASOC cell had no direct communications to the strike aircraft. The fire support cell chief for a SOF contingent, said:

> ...we would call the CAOC, and they would talk to the fighters on UHF [ultra-high frequency]. The distances made it non-standard. We could not talk to the fighters directly because of the huge distances. We had to coordinate it through means that were inefficient. [102]

Once priorities were determined, the ASOC could prioritize strike aircraft and task them to GFAC targets, but it had to rely on the CAOC and its various resources to complete the tasking. The CAOC alone had the rest of the picture – of tanker status, carrier deck cycle times, and other aircraft in the area – that was essential to keeping strike aircraft available at all times.

The air support system in Afghanistan prior to Operation ANACONDA was unusual but it met mission requirements during Operation ENDURING FREEDOM's first phase. However, those planning Operation ANACONDA failed to see that if stressed, the air request system had weaknesses—lack of visibility, lack of prioritization, and others—that could make it inefficient in surge close air support operations. This was part of a larger failure to anticipate that Operation ANACONDA could turn into an opposed operation. That in turn was based on the continuing estimation that enemy fighters in the Shahi Kot valley would be few in number and would not put up much resistance.

But above all, the tale of the ASOC cell was "a symptom," in General Moseley's words. "The bigger issue here," he said, "is there was never an opportunity to orchestrate and figure out what was needed." he reflected later: "Had we known this was going to go on we would have stood up a full ASOC and moved [the people] to Bagram a week or two weeks ahead of this and then conducted a set of rehearsals with carriers, with the bombers, with the whole thing. And I would have forward-deployed the A-10s," he continued, "so you would have had indigenous quick reactions."[103]

USCENTCOM Approval

The final plan for Operation ANACONDA was briefed by the CFLCC during a VTC with General Franks on 26 February 2002. General Franks approved the plan. General Mikolashek then asked General Franks to hear comments from the CFACC, General Moseley. The CAOC had run a quick analysis of air support a few days earlier, and General Moseley said, "I made the point to the CINC [combatant commander], I could probably run two simultaneous CAS events, given the size of that [area].[104] General Moseley told General Franks during the VTC that "given a certain set of considerations" the air component was ready to execute. But this assumed "deconfliction and orchestration of fires" plus knowing the airlift sustainment requirement, approving pre-planned targets, understanding the ROE inside and outside engagement zones, defining ODA and OGA activities, the status and equipment of ETACs and GFACs and more. As General Moseley said in the VTC, "If everybody's got all that ready and can forward that data, and give us a chance to orchestrate this and incorporate it, then I'll be ready to execute on the 28th." Acknowledging the gaps, General Franks commented: "We have some due-outs."[105] The true situation, it was about to be discovered, was considerably less promising. The CFACC staff started working the critical issues, and "it was apparent we didn't have any of that," noted General Moseley.[106]

Later that day, 26 February 2002, the weather intervened. Forecasts of low visibility led to a weather delay because the assault helicopters could not operate safely in low visibility conditions. The two-day slip gave Bagram time to work more problem areas—such as identifying targets.

Targets for Preliminary Airstrikes

Preliminary airstrikes did not figure in the original plan for Operation ANACONDA. As CJTF *Mountain* later explained, he felt airstrikes would be most effective against fixed targets, but few could be found. Hagenback recalled:

> Early on, there were few, if any, fixed targets we could identify as being high-value. We templated (sic) a couple…I did not want to attack the dozens and dozens of cave complexes arbitrarily without having some sense of what was in them.[107]

SOF personnel began to identify targets like "Dishkas" in the Shahi Kot valley. The Russian-made 12.7 or 14.5mm truck-mounted DShKs were a potential threat. Analysis indicated that 20 were in the area. On this basis CJTF *Mountain* nominated several targets, including caves and a ridgeline, to be struck in advance. On 27 February 2002 an Annex to the FRAGO of the OPORD sent forward CJTF *Mountain*'s seven targets for possible pre-planned strikes, including two cave entrances and a "bomber box" of coordinates along a ridge line in a position to threaten helicopter LZs.

To the CFLCC-Fwd staff, these targets were well within the rules of engagement and from very reliable reporting. However, the seven targets "were immediately challenged" and fed into the target vetting process established by USCENTCOM.

"The process developed early in the campaign relied heavily on technical means to support target nominations," noted the CFLCC's after-action report, whereas some of the targets had been spotted by human sources on the ground, creating a disconnect. The net result was that the seven targets did not have all the supporting documentation required—so the decision on pre-planned strikes would have to be worked.[108] "As it turned out, there were about 66 or so pre-surveyed, mensurated coordinate-droppable targets of either cave adits, mortar positions or things like that we could have done some really good work on with JDAMs or GBUs," General Moseley later said.[109]

The cave targets were approved and assigned to F-15Es carrying BLU-118 thermobaric bombs. The other CFLCC-Fwd targets—the bomber box—had not been approved by the time Operation ANACONDA was due to start. According to General Corley, the late approvals meant that the CAOC was not able to plan in advance "the right munition from the right aircraft sequenced in at the right time," instead they had to pass target coordinates to bombers already airborne for most of the first strikes.[110]

Airlift Requirements

The CAOC's air mobility division (AMD) had not been involved in initial planning either. At the CAOC Brigadier General Winfield Scott, U.S. Air Force, and the Director of Mobility Forces (DIRMOBFOR), said he did not "remember the AMD [Air Mobility Division] ever seeing the plan" until the requirement itself appeared.[111]

Yet CJTF *Mountain*'s plan was heavily dependent on airlift support. Among other tasks, they needed to move 700-1,000 soldiers from Kandahar to Bagram. According to the DIRMOBFOR:

> We were allocating X amount of C-130s to meet that lift. At the same time, the fuel situation at Bagram to support the Army aviation was very critical. There was essentially no land support to Bagram.[112]

After the initial build-up, airlift would have to sustain the fuel levels, bring in ammunition, evacuate casualties and deliver any other equipment and supplies needed.

C-17 Globemaster III Offloading Cargo and Fuel at Bagram

To build up and sustain the U.S. Army at Bagram, "We gathered up every available flying resource that we could in that part of the world," said General Corley, including some of the Vice President's C-17s being used for his trip to the region and Marine [Corps] KC-130s.[113]

Fuel reserves for U.S. Army and SOF helicopter operations were limited at Bagram, so the U.S. Army brought in another empty fuel bladder, doubling capacity. To fill it, General Scott used C-17 Globemaster IIIs. "We had a tanker overhead. The C-17 would spiral up, plug in, get the gas, spiral back down and offload gas," he said. Now two of the five dedicated C-17s in theater were being used for "nothing but gas," General Scott said.[114] Other requirements filtered in late, too. The Air Expeditionary Control Team, responsible for aeromedical evacuation, got word of the Operation ANACONDA requirement only four days before it began.

Airlift was being rebalanced to build up CJTF *Mountain* at Bagram. The U.S. Air Force moved several thousand gallons of gas between the 23rd and 28th, of which zero was moved by ground.

During the weather delay, U.S. Army forces continued rehearsals for their operations. At the ASOC, the Assistant Division ALO helped complete the process of getting the 10th Mountain Division staff and all LNOs (for example, from Special Forces units) into one working area at the JOC, which would be CJTF *Mountain*'s command center for the operation.

Ten days was not much time to work through coordination issues and meld three components—SOF, land, and air—into a unified whole. The Bagram ASOC cell was now functional thanks in part to the weather delay. On 1 March 2002, the ASOC cell ran through a battle drill with the air support personnel, ground staff, and LNOs. It did not go well. "Nobody responded, nobody said a word," stated the Assistant Division ALO. They didn't know what to do. "It was very shocking to the Army staff," the Assistant Division ALO said. "If (the first day, 2 March 2002) had gone on the 28th, they'd have been in for a rude awakening." After the poor start, they ran several rehearsals in the remaining hours and "everybody was ready to go (2 March 2002)."[115]

Word of impending action did indeed seep out. On 1 March 2002, reports came that some Afghan soldiers had resigned from units working with U.S. forces in Paktia province. "Most gave family matters as a reason; some [were] concerned about threats to their lives from al-Qaeda for working with U.S. forces, and others gave no reason. None spoke of "any threats against them or the U.S."[116]

Chapter Four

The First 72 Hours: 2 – 4 March 2002

Preparations for Operation ANACONDA began in late February 2002 with SOF teams reconnoitering the area, setting up positions and assisting in getting Afghan military forces in place. 2 March 2002 formally marked the beginning of Operation ANACONDA.

Pre-Assault Activity

AC-130 gunships surveyed the air assault landing zones on the night of 1-2 March 2002 to detect and strike enemy activity, but found nothing and departed as dawn approached. One gunship reported no activity along the prospective line of advance of the Afghan forces. Another gunship reported that the blocking positions along the northern landing zones were clear near Blocking Positions (BPs) *Amy, Betty, Cindy* and *Diane*, although the crew reported some "hot" buildings and a group of people moving on a path. But this gunship could not continue on to reconnoiter the southern blocking positions "due to a maintenance problem."[117] Although no one knew it, the hottest spot in Operation ANACONDA had just been overlooked.

Next came airstrikes on the east and west sides of the Shahi Kot valley. An F-15E dropped a BLU-118 thermobaric bomb on a mountain cave site. JDAMS were used to hit cave areas in a box along the back of a prominent foothill ridge soon to be known as "the whale."[118]

The CFLCC-Fwd had requested strikes on these targets to close caves and suppress enemy forces. However, the preparatory strike was not completed as planned.

SOF teams inserted earlier were not briefed on the pre-assault air strikes. Despite efforts at the CAOC to deconflict, "a lot of the targets they [CJTF *Mountain*] picked [nominated to the CAOC]" were close to SOF teams.[119] As bombs started to fall, teams on the ground were uninformed of the preplanned fires and believed they were being fired on by friendlies, which resulted in them broadcasting a "knock it off" request part way through the strike. Friendly aircrews broke off their attacks.[120]

The attack on Objective *Remington* began in two phases. First, Afghan forces, dubbed "Hammer", were to move south and enter the lower valley area from both the northern and southern approaches while closing in on Objective *Remington*. The Afghan forces began moving down the road toward Serhkhankel, the entry point to the Shahi Kot valley. Already in place were the two other groups of Afghan forces serving as the "Anvil." One group was at the lower end of the valley, north of Urgun, and another was on the other side of the mountains near Khowst effectively blocking escape routes to the south and east.

Then the plan started to unravel. The northern groups of Afghan forces – the hammer – were hit with what they thought was heavy indirect mortar fire about 3 nm from Objective Remington. Two soldiers were killed outright and five wounded. One of the two killed was Cobra 72, Warrant Officer Stanley Harriman, U.S. Army, the air controller with the ground forces. The attack was later determined to be accidental fire from an AC-130.[121] Shortly thereafter the Afghan Commander elected to return to Gardez to obtain more vehicles and re-arm, noting he might continue operations the next day. As General Franks put it: "the determination was made by that Afghan force that they needed to pull back a few kilometers, regroup, get new vehicles, organize themselves and so forth, which they did."[122]

Air Assault by TF *Rakkasan*

The operation continued to unfold as "Hammer" forces retreated. Next came the air assault by "Anvil."

AH-64 Apache helicopters made a pass through the valley floor to clear the way for the air assault troops and suppress fire at the landing zones. Shortly thereafter the 101st Airborne Division's 2-187 Infantry assaulted blocking positions to the north on the foothills between the upper and lower Shahi Kot valley. This first wave of air assault forces all made it into the landing zone and to their blocking positions. But enemy fire was intense. "Flew in to LZ [landing zone]... Under fire when we stepped off the helicopter," one GFAC noted.[123]

Another air assault wave, bringing in the 10th Mountain Division's 1-87 Infantry Battalion, headed for the three southern blocking positions. They took BP *Eve* and *Heathe*r but "BP *Ginger* had a heavy concentration of enemy." The soldiers landed "at the base of an al-Qaeda stronghold and literally within a minute of being dropped off began taking sporadic fires as they moved to cover." Troops were under fire all morning. The site for the Battalion command center was also under fire and the forces committed to those sites relocated to an alternate landing zone north of *Ginger*.[124] "I didn't really expect them to try and duke it out with us," said the 1-187th Infantry Battalion Commander. "I was just surprised at the intensity of what I saw on the valley floor."[125]

As those landing near BP *Ginger* found, the heaviest concentration of enemy resistance was near Marzak. One small hamlet to the south of Marzak, had 50 enemy troops with mortars. Rotary and fixed-wing air support were used for all indirect fires. AH-64 Apaches delivered fires but were damaged by RPGs and small arms crossfire.[126]

A Sergeant Major with the 1-87th Infantry, 10th Mountain Division, led the southern air assault. He brought in troops on CH-47s to blocking positions about 400 meters apart. "The intent was that the Afghan forces, after we set our blocking position, would sweep through the villages and dislodge any al-Qaeda in the villages," the Sergeant Major said. But "the picture intel painted was just a little bit different than the actual events happening on the ground," he said. "Basically my element to the south landed right at the base of an al-Qaeda stronghold." The Sergeant Major noted mortar fire, RPGs, heavy machine gun fire, light machine gun fire and small arms fire from the hills above his troops' position. At the start of the firefight "within the first 30 minutes or so" they called in close air support. "That quieted things down," he said.[127]

The first CAS strike came when a B-52 released JDAMs on targets designated by controllers in the early morning hours. Within an hour, a B-52 hit a building in Marzak with JDAMs. A few minutes later a B-52 dropped on troops in the open with a string of 500-pound bombs.[128]

Calls for close air support continued throughout the day. The Assistant Division ALO at Bagram described the immediate CAS tasking from the ASOC perspective:

> It was nuts. It was non-stop and it went for about 24 hours. A lot of our guys, the ones who were in close combat for about 18 hours. We pushed them everything we had. They got B-52s, F-15s. As night fell, the gunships came back on station.[129]

The ASOC monitored GFAC requests for support. Strike aircraft contacted AWACS. AWACS then sent the aircraft into designated orbit points and handed them off to the ETAC selected by the ASOC. (On the first day, some ETACs, had to contact AWACS directly due to communications problems with the ASOC.)

To keep track of requests, the ASOC set up a Plexiglas board. With grease pencils "we wrote down all the sorties that were in their vul [vulnerability] periods so we could track who was on the tanker, who was executed, whom we tasked, whatever." The Assistant Division ALO reported that they often had three or four troops-in-contact situations at once "and they just kept coming. We would sequence aircraft in one after another."[130]

Four B-1 aircrews who worked the Shahi Kot valley on 2 March 2002 carried out a range of missions, each directly responsive to ground controllers requests. At mid-morning, a B-1 released JDAMs on troops and ridgeline targets for one controller, and then extended their vulnerability period significantly to drop more JDAMs for a second controller. In the early afternoon, another B-1, over a two-hour period, released 19 JDAMs on ten different targets for multiple ground controllers. At 1600 local time, an additional B-1 delivered a box pattern of instantaneous fused JDAMs and worked other targets including a "Zeus [ZSU-23 23mm antiaircraft artillery piece] coming out of a cave" spotted by the controller. Another B-1 mission reported they "dropped a total of 15 GBU-31s on six targets during six separate bomb runs."[131]

Deconfliction got sticky. A B-52, dropped GBU-31s on Marzak at 1828 local time under control of a GFAC, then positioned for another run to release a string of MK-82s. The bomber was 30 seconds from the launch window when another GFAC asked the bomber crew if they "could see the AC-130 below them." They couldn't – and with just 10 seconds to go, the aircraft commander wisely "decided to withhold weapons." The B-52 refueled and returned for another strike, only to be called off by the CAOC due to medical evacuation activity in the area.[132]

By late afternoon, CJTF *Mountain* assessed that "hard-core elements, sensing success against Coalition forces, perceive no need to exfiltrate at this time." Mortar attacks from the Marzak area continued into the evening as enemy forces regenerated mortar positions and conducted "traditional *Mujaheddin* hit and run tactics."[133] Marzak had been hit already, but CJTF *Mountain* declared later that evening the entire village of Marzak hostile.[134] Questions were raised at the CAOC when the request to hit Marzak came through because of the USCENTCOM ROE, but USCENTCOM confirmed that "if CJTF *Mountain* declared it hostile, you can strike it," General Corley recalled.[135]

The first day of Operation ANACONDA brought mixed results. The northern blocking positions were under pressure but in place. Coalition Special Forces and the Afghan forces at Khowst maintained the outer cordon. However, by 1700 local time, CJTF *Mountain* knew they were facing a more difficult fight. Their newest estimate described 200-300 al-Qaeda forces still in the area around the three villages, with up to 100 more in the surrounding hills. Commanders soon knew they were facing not just Taliban and al-Qaeda, but also other foreign fighters in the area.[136] CJTF *Mountain* reported, "The enemy positions on Takur Gar and Marzak are presenting robust defenses."[137]

CJTF *Mountain* elected to extract troops from the southern positions and reinforce the northern BPs. Along with the conventional forces, a SOF team was also extracted from positions near a ridge called Takur Gar. This decision would have unintended consequences a few days later when it came time to try to reinsert the team.

For now, the first day was almost over. One SITREP that evening concluded: "Enemy continues to control the high ground in vic [in the vicinity of] whaleback and small fortified pockets throughout the area of operations."[138] An AC-130 covered a helicopter evacuating casualties. When an al-Qaeda mortar landed near the helicopter, the AC-130 observed the mortar launch, pinpointed the location and fired, killing two to three personnel.[139]

The AH-64 Apache helicopters engaged in the fight all took damage. By the end of the day, four returned to the forward arming and refueling point (FARP), while three remained in action despite battle damage. Bagram sent one additional AH-64 to the FARP. CJTF *Mountain* requested immediate deployment of additional AH-64s to Kandahar and contacted the Combined Force Maritime Component Commander (CFMCC) for "immediate tactical control (TACON)" of AH-1 Cobras embarked on a nearby amphibious ship.[140]

Perceptions of Operation ANACONDA after 2 March 2002

The intense fight surprised both ground and air commanders. In fact, the enemy response was turning out to be closer to the worst-case scenario of "defense in depth" postulated in the initial OPORD. CJTF *Mountain* described how well the enemy had prepared. "We found mortar base plates that were cemented in, allowing the al Qaeda [sic] to move tubes easily in and out of the caves," he said in a later interview. "They already had registered their mortars on the key pieces of terrain and other features throughout the valley."[141]

The first day's operations also exposed stress points in the command and organization of Coalition forces. Operation ANACONDA's true air support requirements were nothing like previous Operation ENDURING FREEDOM experience or the initial plan in CJTF *Mountain's* CONOPS. Instead of dropping bombs over several hotspots across the whole of Afghanistan, nearly all the requests were called to drop within small areas where over 35 ETACs were estimated to be in place.[142] In comparison, a U.S. Army division operating on a traditional, conventional battlefield might have 1/5 as many ETACs in an area the same size.

Plenty of air support was available. "I was always excess to need in terms of available strikes to support the requests of CJTF *Mountain*," General Corley said later.[143] But the unexpected demand for close air support coupled with the deficiencies of the theater air control system was a jolt. SOF teams were operating very close to conventional forces.

With the tight airspace crowding strike aircraft closer together than ever before, many of the aircrews had hair-raising stories to tell about near misses. Others ran out of time while aircraft ahead of them worked targets. At the CAOC, the Chief of Combat Operations had left at H-4 [H-hour minus four hours], but when he came back the next morning, "everybody was shell-shocked," he said. "I hadn't seen people's faces like that at all from the entire time we'd entered the fight."[144]

At the ASOC, the Assistant Division ALO and his team worked straight through, all the while assigning priorities and helping to deconflict requests. By the end of the day they felt "like we had just accomplished a historic victory in airpower and [were] really proud of ourselves," he recalled. Multiple requests for close air support had been filled and forward air controllers attested to the success of the strikes. However, there was no coherent picture of the ground situation indicating what had been accomplished. While the ASOC thought they had met the challenge, CJTF *Mountain* was dissatisfied. "The next thing that happened was the U.S. Army leadership came over and was berating us about the lack of close air support," reported the Assistant Division ALO.[145]

To the CFLCC-Fwd staff, Operation ANACONDA was a "new" tactical environment where friendly troops were under fire from "areas, not precise points." U.S. Army planners chafed at having to transmit precision coordinates in order to employ JDAMs. In fact, the whole concept of precision coordinate bombing seemed at odds with what the CFLCC-Fwd wanted many times during the battle. The CFLCC-Fwd's perspective was that the precision bombing process slowed down close air support and delayed vital suppressive fires. For the first 48 hours "CFLCC-Fwd struggles to defeat the Operation ENDURING FREEDOM mindset of DMPI-level data required to employ air delivered munitions in the close battle," remarked the CJTF *Mountain* report to CFLCC.[146] The impression persisted. A CFLCC-Fwd summary of the battle later stated: "From that first contact, we struggled to break the paradigm of point targeting in order to achieve the immediate desired effect."[147]

Reports from the ground forward air controllers reflected a different picture: overall satisfaction with airpower. For example, B-52s and B-1s, delivered air support on 2 March 2002. One single controller team tasked B-1s to strike targets that day. Many of the bomber targets attacked with JDAMs and with MK-82s against "troops in open" or mortar firing positions. On top of that were the U.S. Navy and Air Force fighter sorties. Controllers sometimes had to work with the aircrews to fine-tune weapons delivery, but the overall effect was that the bombs had to be delivered where and when the controllers on the ground needed them to go.

Two early incidents perhaps colored Bagram's perspective on airpower. One was the frustration surrounding Marzak. When Marzak was declared a hostile area, one of the strikes was a B-52 releasing GBU-31s on "buildings in Marzak."[148] Ground Controllers passed precision coordinates and got fast "suppressive fires" effects.

The second incident was frustration over failing to hit a truck observed on Predator video. Watching a live Predator feed, the JOC at Bagram spotted a truck behind the battle lines that appeared to be re-supplying enemy forces and ordered it killed. CJTF *Mountain* told the ASOC cell to blow up the truck. The ASOC told him they had troops-in-contact requests but he reiterated the order. "We tried to send several sets of fighters at it," the Assistant Division ALO attested. As he told the story two months later:

> ...this truck was a flatbed, stake-bed truck driving through a ravine up in the hills, in the vicinity of but not in the heat of battle...the first aircraft they sent over there were F-16s and ... they couldn't find them so they ran out of gas. Everybody is tensely awaiting to see this thing blow up on TV. Then when I said, 'Sorry, gotta roll another set of fighters in there.' You know everybody was just so pissed.... We had another set of F-18s, sent them in, bottom line, never hit it....[149]

The ALO remembered that the commander came over to him and said: "'Do I have to call in air myself: Who do I need to talk to on this phone?' He picks up the hotline, he's screaming and hollering, trying to talk to the CAOC..."[150] This story, recalled from the heat of battle, vividly conveyed the sense of frustration with the air control system and uncertainty over the rules of engagement.

The truck was difficult to find without a FAC in place to pass along the coordinates and help talk the aircraft onto the target. "I think that event triggered the attitude that we were not providing close air support," said the Assistant Division ALO.

Frustration aside, the fundamental issue remained about the propriety of diverting strike assets from troops-in-contact (TIC) to chase a truck. He summarized that the Predator's live feed "stared at that truck for hours …It was a waste of an asset that could have helped defend guys, could have helped with other targeting."[151]

The dramatic failure to hit the truck was carried out in clear view, because of the live Predator feed to the JOC. In contrast, there was no complete, real-time picture of the results of the day's CAS strikes available to CJTF *Mountain* or other commanders. CAS results were measured by ground controllers' comments, generally to the pilots themselves. The full picture of requests filled, ordnance delivered, and al-Qaeda knocked out of action could only emerge later in aggregate databases, controllers' after action reports, and the pilot mission reports. At Bagram, in the heat of battle—as at Camp Doha or Prince Sultan Air Base—it was hard to gauge the cumulative impact.

In fact, the joint air component delivered 177 precision bombs (JDAM GBU-31s and laser-guided 500-pound GBU-12s) in the first 24 hours. Of these, 162 were immediate CAS responses—firepower delivered from sorties catalogued as XCAS (airborne alert CAS) on the ATO and responding to immediate ground force requests for strikes. The precision weapons delivered for immediate CAS averaged out to over six bombs per hour, or one every ten minutes. Actual drops ebbed and flowed with the ground situation. Afternoon was the peak time with 64 precision weapons released by bombers and fighters from 1300 to 1800 local time. Two B-52s dropped strings of 27 MK-82s on troops in the open and on a ridgeline for a total of 54 MK-82s dropped on 2 March 2002, all as immediate CAS. Two F/A-18Cs strafed enemy firing positions, making three passes and delivering 400 rounds of 20mm cannon apiece as darkness closed in at around 1730 local time. That night, AC-130 gunships flew three orbits over the battle area, attacking targets with 40mm and 105mm guns and passing DMPIs to other strikers.[152]

3 March 2002

"Today we tightened the circle around Objective Remington" by reinforcing the task forces, closing exfiltration routes by repositioning several teams, "and conducting several airstrikes against enemy vehicles and personnel," CJTF *Mountain* reported to CFLCC on 3 March 2002.[153]

With no sign that Afghan forces were ready to take up the "Hammer" task again, CJTF *Mountain* sent in his reserve to regain some of the momentum of the attack. On 3 March 2002, the first serial ground forces of the 101st Airborne Division air assaulted in with a small force of approximately 50+ soldiers. But the second serial aborted "due to hot LZ." They went in ten hours later, after dark, at around midnight local time. "Battle continues…fighting off enemy resistance consisting mostly of harassing mortar and small arms fire," the nightly operational report summarized. "Once again, near continuous use of CAS assets and only enough for TIC situations," it continued.[154] The troops of 10th Mountain Division continued to experience mortar fire 'from sun up to sun down.

Infiltration and exfiltration of special operations teams—including many Coalition forces—continued throughout the first two days of the battle. For example, one Coalition team was compromised by a local mob throwing rocks at them. Twenty minutes later they requested exfiltration.

Forces on the ground were still under heavy fire. Marzak and Babulkyel were bombed, the latter with a B-1 and a B-52 strike. Close air support hit mortar positions and caves.[155] "Numerous bombing strikes were made against dug-in enemy forces in Babulkeyl nearby resulting in moderate to heavy enemy casualties," CJTF *Mountain* reported.[156]

Two Airmen from the 19 ASOS experienced the intensity of the battle on the ground. One described his experience:

> We moved with C Company to the north to a bowl where we took mortar, sniper, and machinegun (DShK) fire. We moved from ridge to ridge trying to avoid the bad situation. We kept just in front of their rounds. While this was happening the TAC [terminal attack controller] was unsuccessful in knocking out the mortar fire. So I told my partner to stay and request aircraft. I took his plugger [GPS receiver] and the [laser range finder]. I went to the top of the hill and got the exact grid to the mortar position. We did all this while mortar fire was coming down on and around our position. An aircraft was diverted to our position almost instantaneously. We gave them the coordinates and they dropped bombs, knocking out the mortar position. We did the exact same for the Dishka as they dropped more bombs. The last target was the mortar position to our southeast, on a ridge. We called for another aircraft and had the B-52s drop bombs on the ridge. That night the TAC sent the battle captain to get us and move us to the Bn [battalion] TOC [Fire Base Raider]. We rucked [hiked carrying ruck sacks] to their position; met with the battalion commander and rucked with him all night long to link up with the battalion being air assaulted in the morning.[157]

Objective Ginger still remained out of reach. Plans called for troops to start clearing the eastern ridgeline from north to south the next morning. This pocket of al-Qaeda and Taliban forces were well-prepared to resist.

Battle at Takur Gar (Roberts Ridge)

Before TF *Rakkasan*'s renewed operations got underway, special operations forces made an attempt to put a team into the area near Objective *Ginger*, evacuated by

1-87 Infantry on the first night. A chain of events led to seven casualties before the day was out.

The decision to extract conventional and SOF troops on night one from the southern blocking positions and Objective *Ginger* left a key vantage point unmanned. As a senior military official later described it, Objective *Ginger* was just below a mountaintop known as Takur Gar. Retaking the ridge was essential to taking Objective *Ginger* and completing the US conventional forces' portion of the campaign. "This OP position that we were putting in up on top of that hill had a commanding view of not only Ginger but also that entire valley," the official said. Takur Gar offered 15 miles of visibility across the battlespace in good weather – perfect for observing ground troops and conducting Type I CAS talk-ons.[158]

The resistance encountered by the Sergeant Major of the 1-87th Infantry and other troops on day one indicated the al-Qaeda were dug in around Objective *Ginger* and well-supplied. There needed to be a SOF team on the mountaintop to control airstrikes and perform other functions before the renewed conventional offensive to take Objective *Ginger*. Said the senior military official: "…that was significant terrain to us and the enemy thought so, too."[159]

The reinsertion of a special operations team began early morning hours of 4 March 2002.[160] One of two MH-47s was hit by three RPGs while attempting to re-insert the team, damaging hydraulic systems. In an attempt to withdraw hastily while under intense fire, the first MH-47 rapidly lifted off, and Petty Officer First Class Neil C. Roberts, a U.S. Navy SEAL fell from the aircraft. He activated his infrared strobe light and returned fire on the enemy but was soon captured and killed by al-Qaeda forces.

That first MH-47 made it about 4 nm north of the landing zone before being forced down with mechanical problems. Its troops and aircrew were picked up by the second MH-47, and flown to FARP Gardez. Once they reached the FARP, they unloaded wounded personnel and six special operations personnel returned by helicopter "to rescue their mate."[161]

A second rescue force was also on the way. By 0515 local time, two helicopters carrying Rangers from the Quick Reaction Force (QRF) at Bagram were en route to assist recovery of the individual missing in action. Then at 0540 local time, the lead MH-47 from the QRF, was hit by RPG fire. The helicopter was following a flight path similar to the first two helicopters a few hours earlier. On board were nine U.S. Army Rangers, two U.S. Air Force pararescue jumpers (PJ), and eight aircrew members from the 160th Special Operations Aviation Regiment (Airborne). A U.S. Air Force Staff Sergeant said:

> At 0140Z [0610 local time] I had noticed we were flying in circles around the mountaintop because I had noticed the same terrain twice. As we were circling about the third time, we were hit with a rocket-propelled grenade around 0145Z [0715 local time]. There were sparks on the right side of the aircraft and we started to shake violently. Then our helicopter just fell out of the sky about 15 feet to the ground.[162]

The first three crew members to exit the back of the helicopter were killed by small arms fire from al-Qaeda defensive positions.

Veering off quickly, the second QRF helicopter landed safely about a kilometer away. But Takur Gar was a sheer face. This new position meant the second QRF team with 10 Rangers now had a 3,000-foot vertical climb to reach the crash site.[163] Until the QRF or other help could reach them, the ambushed force on the ground with dead and wounded had to rely on its own firepower and on close air support to hold off the enemy.

"There was ample close air support in the area," said the military official, an Army aviator.[164] However, a two-ship flight of F-15Es arrived and remained on station from about 0405 to 0730 local time. After working one call from a controller on the west side of the whale, AWACS vectored the F-15Es over to assist the self-rescue effort. The F-15Es released two GBU-12s against a mortar position, getting a hit with the second bomb. The AWACS then pulled the F-15Es out for refueling and directed a B-52 into the area.

The B-52 crew was orbiting when they were contacted by a FAC. As the B-52 crew was on their run to the designated coordinates, the GFAC, part of the rescue team and on the ground, called them off due to friendlies in the area. The refueled F-15Es were directed to release 11 bombs near the whale. Then the GFAC contacted them and directed the F-15Es to strafe on a southwest heading.

The F-15E's first run was called off by GFAC. He corrected the heading, and the F-15E strafed at 0720 local time. A third run at 0721 local time was right on top of the al-Qaeda troops according to the GFAC as was another run at 0723 local time. Each run expended between 80-180 of the 20mm PGU-28 rounds. Following the pattern, the second F-15E rolled in several minutes later and strafed with four runs at 0743, 0746, 0748, and 0750 local times to suppress enemy troop movement.[165]

But the day was just beginning for the GFAC, who had to help protect wounded troops and rescuers on the ground until they could be evacuated. Two F-16CGs were now in the area. He requested the F-16 strafe at 0807 and make a second run at 0810 local times, using up all of this F-16's 20mm ammunition. The strafing was too far down the ridgeline. The other F-16CG made one strafing pass at 0824 and came around again at 0826 local time.

At 0841 local time a B-52 dropped one JDAM on a command post and another on a mortar position on the ridge. The F-15E flight refueled then held due to Predator activity in the area. Once released, they returned to drop their last GBU-12s. At 0929 the F-15E had a hung bomb, but shortly after the second aircraft released its GBU-12 at 0934 local time. The GFAC wanted a bomb 300 meters north-northwest of where the last bomb hit, and the F-15E delivered the bomb only 200 meters from the downed helicopter. Shortly thereafter the F-16s returned to employ their GBU-12s.

The F-16's returned to employ their GBU-12s. The successes of these missions represented the best in XCAS; the experience of one B-52 aircrew did not. The B-52 under a GFAC's control was ready with a MK-82 strike as requested when they were called off. Over the next few hours, the aircraft was moved off due to airspace deconfliction problems, sent back in with new targets, waived off once more, asked to switch from MK-82s to JDAMs, and then to switch back again to higher-priority MK-82 targets. Their final try at a strike failed that evening when an AC-130 gunship could not be cleared from the airspace below them. This flight was whipsawed by divergent guidance from the ground controller to the CAOC controllers. "After over three hours in the target area and ten separate targeting attempts, the B-52 crew returned to base with all twelve JDAM and 27 MK-82s," their MISREP [mission report] for their 15-hour mission reported.[166]

Half of a U.S. Navy four-ship of F/A-18s had the same experience. At 1745 local time, they responded to a ground controller's call by dropping 5 GBU-12s on three target areas, one of which was about 200 meters to the east of friendly positions. AWACS tasked the other half of the package to contact the GFAC, then a call sign used by the Predator, then yet another controller. None of this resulted in strikes and the F/A-18s were finally instructed "to hold overhead the helo crash site and await tasking," they reported. "No tasking was passed."[167]

On the whole, close air support worked well for the trapped forces that day. The GFAC at the crash site estimated that he controlled about 30 CAS sorties that day before being extracted. The 682ASOS Commander described the CAS as "a timely and smooth flow." He said, "We kept bullets and bombs on the enemy pretty much for the next 15 hours."[168] It was also plenty close. One ETAC later reported that weapons were dropped from as close as 100 meters to no more than 300 meters away. "They dropped one at 100 meters and this huge piece of flaming metal flew over our heads, went halfway down the hill, blew up and started a big fire. We thought that was a little close," the ETAC later said.[169]

CAS continued throughout the day, as did combat on the ground at Takur Gar. There "were multiple enemy all around this mountain-top, coming and going," said a senior military official. U.S. Army Rangers were attacked from behind at one point.[170] But their skill and bravery held off the better-positioned enemy force. Late that morning, the QRF Team with 10 U.S. Army Rangers climbing from 3,000 feet below made it to the top and linked up with the others on the ridge. Around noon, they assaulted and took the al-Qaeda positions near the crash site.[171] It was estimated 40-50 enemy killed in action (KIA) during the daylight battle.[172] At about 1630 local time, personnel found the body of the U.S. Navy SEAL, and reported him KIA. The 38 personnel at Takur Gar were extracted by 2045 local time.

Improving Close Air Support

By 4 March 2002, the CFACC had taken several steps to improve the flow of air support to the ongoing operations. "Day one or day two, I'm not happy now with what we're seeing," General Moseley recalled. First, the CFACC and CFLCC spoke about areas of concern, including the "absolute requirement" for better target ID and target coordinates, generating additional strike targets, prioritizing CAS, and the problems caused because not all GFACs had the equipment to determine precise target coordinates.

Some quick solutions were put in place. First, General Moseley sent the incoming USCENTAF/A-3 Chief of the Strategy Cell, an experienced A-10 pilot, to Bagram to augment the ASOC cell. "Because the ASOC doesn't work for the Army, they work for me," he said. "That made me even madder. Not only were we not able to get [them] there, but when we got it up there, we didn't have it right," he said. General Moseley also suggested that the U.S. Army Colonel, Chief of the BCD get himself up to Bagram to help out, too. They arrived at Bagram on 5 March 2002 and called back to tell General Moseley the situation was "worse than you thought."[173]

Second, the CFACC also adjusted ordnance loads for strike aircraft pushed to Operation ANACONDA to include close air support weapons such as CBU-87s and air-burst MK-82s.[174]

Third, A-10s were temporarily based closer to the operation.[175] The A-10 detachment would provide both dedicated close air support and FAC-A capabilities to help deconflict strike aircraft working over the Operation ANACONDA battle area.[176]

The first two A-10s, made a five-hour flight from Kuwait and arrived over the battle area at sunset to hear "two or three different ground FACs screaming for emergency CAS." The two-ship was pushed to the GFAC from 10th Mountain Division. He had inserted on 2 March 2002 with the 1-87 Infantry then moved 8 km to an overwatch position, which made contact with the enemy at about 1600 local time.[177] One A-10 pilot stated:

> These guys were apparently under fire with heavy machine gun and mortars. They needed to get fire on these guys immediately, so we showed up. It was extremely hard to make anything of the battlefield. It was just dark down there. You could see tracer fire and pockets of fire all over the place.[178]

The two A-10s released MK-82 bombs set for airburst to hit enemy troops at the mortar position at 1817 local time. After the attack, "the ground FAC said that all the fire they were taking ceased and that it looked like we whacked these guys out in the open. There wasn't much movement out there anymore." "Targets and personnel neutralized," the GFAC recorded. Pulling up from one pass, an A-10 came within 300 yards of an orbiting gunship. Later, the A-10s were surprised when F/A-18s dropped weapons underneath them. The traffic convinced them "we were probably going to have to take a more proactive role in our other primary job which is forward air control."[179]

Adding to the uncertainty, intelligence reports indicated that more reinforcements might be on the way. "An unknown factor is the number of enemy apparently moving into the Shahi Kot valley from both the northeast and south," CJTF *Mountain* noted. "Unconfirmed reports indicate up to 400 personnel are en route to Shahi Kot from the

Ghazni province," to the west. After the third day of battle, CJTF *Mountain's* report to CFLCC on 4 March 2002 revised the number of al-Qaeda fighters in the area. "Our revised estimate of forces faced during (the first day, 2 march 2002) is approximately 400-500 personnel," the report stated.[180]

Assessing the First 72 Hours

There was no doubt at CJTF *Mountain* that the al-Qaeda and Taliban forces were taking casualties. Reports to the CFLCC on enemy killed climbed to 353 (230 confirmed and 123 probable) after the first four days of Operation ANACONDA.[181] According to CJTF *Mountain*, enemy fighters were "staggering from three nights of airstrikes and facing new daylight strikes."[182]

The air component contributed far more than the predicted two simultaneous CAS events at a time "but we did it at extremely high risk to our folks," General Moseley later said. "We ended up dropping bombs through orbits. We simultaneously attacked sites from adjacent ground parties with not the right amount of comfort with ingressing and egressing fighters, all while taking weapons fire and surface-to-air missiles or MANPAD fire through all of this," he added.[183]

The inability to clarify "fires" procedures and the unique ROE as well as tactics, techniques, and procedures (TTP) before Operation ANACONDA took its toll. One report later concluded that "plans for the operation did not account for an immediate transition from a deliberate strike scenario to [a] forces in contact scenario."[184]

Despite this, the tally of airstrikes was significant. In the first 72 hours, 751 bombs fell into the Operation ANACONDA battle area (495 precision strikes and 256 MK-82s). Of those, 674 were immediate CAS, with the rest falling on pre-planned targets. Bombers delivered strings of 27 MK-82s five times in 15 hours on 3 March 2002. U.S. Navy and USAF fighters strafed and AC-130 gunships kept up a constant coverage with nine sorties flown in hours of darkness and near-darkness. Statistics showed that bombs fell in 62 of the first 72 hours, making for an even, persistent level of coverage and support to the engaged ground forces. Strike counts were higher in the daytime but continued steadily at night even while AC-130s kept up constant orbits over the battle area.

"My guys have heard me say this a lot: that battlefield…was smaller than the battlefield at Chancellorsville," said General Moseley.[185] As the 18ASOG Commander commented, "We didn't have a theater air control system so we had no discipline in the system and we were trying to institute discipline at the time. Well it's hard to institute discipline when both the Army or the Air Force don't think they need it," he added. At the ASOC cell "the Assistant Division ALO demanded a modicum of discipline or it would have been a complete disaster," the Colonel said.[186]

For both air and ground commanders and staff, there was frustration over the role of the ASOC and the procedures for air requests.

As General Corley later said, "during the early stages, this had been an ill-conceived plan, not properly integrated, not trained, not vetted, not prepared—and then it went horribly bad from minute number one."[187] Quick reactions by soldiers on the ground, persistent close air support, the extraction of forces from BPs *Eve*, *Heather* and *Ginger* and the commitment of the TF *Summit* theater reserve force contained damage and kept Operation ANACONDA underway despite the confusion. "CJTF *Mountain* forces have killed and destroyed a significant number of enemy personnel and materiel through the combined use of air and ground fires," concluded CJTF *Mountain's* nightly report after the first 72 hours.[188] But the task of securing the area and wiping out the concentration of al-Qaeda and Taliban was far from over.

Chapter Five

Renewing the Attack: 5 – 15 March 2002

As the survivors were being extracted from Roberts Ridge, elsewhere CJTF *Mountain* was gearing up for a renewed phase of the offensive to begin on 5 March 2002. It was a change from the 72-hour mindset, and it took into account that the enemy forces present were much stronger than anticipated. "Initially, CFLCC-Fwd estimated 125-200 al-Qaeda fighters in the immediate Shahi Kot area," CJTF *Mountain* noted. "This estimate did not take into account local males who would join the fight or enemy from outside the area reinforcing." Unconfirmed reports still indicated up to 400 personnel might be en route to Shahi Kot valley from Ghazni province to the west. CJTF *Mountain* believed there was still a cluster of about 100-150 al-Qaeda in the southern zone east of Objective *Ginger*. Smaller groups of less than 30 were thought to be in place at pre established checkpoints, on Tergul Ghar (the actual Afghan name for the whale), and on the central and northern ridgelines.[189]

Building Up to Renew the Attack

One of the first requirements for renewing the attack was to bring in more helicopters. Additional AH-64 Apaches were on their way via C-17s from Fort Campbell, Kentucky, to Kandahar, for use in Bagram. Maintenance crews worked to get the battle-damaged AH-64 Apaches back in service as soon as possible, and succeeded in returning several to flying status before Operation ANACONDA ended. Meanwhile, CJTF *Mountain* still needed more helicopters from within the theater.

As requested, the USS *Bonhomme Richard* returned to support the operation. U.S. Marines aboard with the 13th Marine Expeditionary Unit (SOC) Air Combat Element (ACE) flew their AH-1W Cobras and CH-53E Sea Stallions ashore to Bagram airfield where they flew close air support and air assault under CFLCC's TACON for direct support to CJTF *Mountain* for over a week.[190]

A second task was to reactivate Afghani support. An Afghan force moved into positions west of the whale, on the edge of Objective *Remington*, on 4 March 2002. As it turned out, these Afghan forces went back to refit in case of an attack by the reported 400-man al-Qaeda force thought to be on the move from Andar to Zurmat.[191]

A third task was to resupply forces now involved in a protracted fight. Sustainment required airlift, and the DIRMOBFOR, General Scott, found his team reacting to the surging U.S. Army requirements. "They immediately started pushing requirements after the hostilities began," General Scott said. "That became the number one priority—sustaining ANACONDA." Most of the pop-up requirements were for more ammunition. A continual flow of airlift kept troops and supplies moving back and forth from Kandahar to Bagram. The needed sustainment quickly exceeded planning requirements. "We were refragging missions left and right because the requests [for airlift] were coming in too late," he later said. "It took a good week to settle down where we were not in the react mode," General Scott added.[192]

The pieces were now in place to tighten the circle. Reconnaissance teams moved into position to "provide eyes on *Ginger*" and observe the ratline to the southeast, a series of trails through a ravine that was a potential escape route. By the end of the day, SOF estimated that ground controllers had directed "over 30,000-pounds of ordnance dropped on enemy positions" in the operation so far.[193]

The main effort in the renewed attack fell to TF *Rakkasan*. Insertion of one task force by air assault began at 1615 local time on 5 March 2002, with CH-47 Chinooks carrying troops and AH-64 Apaches in support. Other conventional task forces had also been reinforced over the last few days and they now had six 81mm and two 120mm mortars. A radar system for locating indirect fire was to be air assaulted in for them at 0300 local time on 6 March 2002. Plus, "with the addition of two A-10 Thunderbolts, CJTF *Mountain's* ability to kill or destroy the enemy has increased significantly," CJTF *Mountain* reported.[194]

Close air support had helped both TF *Rakkasan* and SOF teams hold on during the first three days. Now, it would strike al-Qaeda concentrations and help close in on the final objectives.

Valley of Death

CJTF *Mountain* expected the al-Qaeda to make a move. The 5 March 2002 report anticipated that "elements already in the Objective *Ginger* AOR will continue their movement into pre-established fighting positions to the south and east." [195]

In a valley to the south, a cluster of troops was doing just that. A series of airstrikes on al-Qaeda reinforcements helped turn the tide on 5 March 2002. Late in the afternoon, a Predator spotted vehicles and al-Qaeda fighters in a ravine to the south of Objective *Ginger*. They appeared to be reinforcements. "They are coming down off the hills and it looks like they are saddling up," recounted one of the pilots later assigned to attack them. Beefed up al-Qaeda and Taliban forces could threaten TF *Summit's* reinforcement and put the plan to secure the last blocking positions in jeopardy.[196]

A ground controller from the 19 ASOS hiked 9 nm the day before to move into position near Objective *Ginger*. He and another controller were with another Coalition special operations unit. They were now in overwatch positions but they could not get "eyes on target." Long afternoon shadows and the terrain made it tough to see into the ravine. Two A-10s were on station and ready to attack but struggled to identify the target because of the difficult lighting conditions.

Fortunately, Predators had significant visibility into the ravine. The A-10s marked the mouth of the valley with a rocket so that the Predator could confirm the location. Late in the afternoon, the two A-10s dropped MK-82 airbursts on the troops in the valley. Then, the lead A-10 took up the FAC-A role and guided two F/A-18s to drop MK-82s on "troops in the open" a few minutes later.[197] After that, according to an A-10 pilot, "we decided to finish it off and add some psychological impacts and then we started strafing them. I put down about 250 rounds of 30mm and then another A-10 pilot put down another 200-250 rounds of 30mm, right into the area just to let them know that we were there, in case anybody was still alive at that point," said the A-10 pilot, from the 74th Expeditionary Fighter Squadron.[198]

Two hours later, two more A-10s unloaded more MK-82s on the target area. A third two-ship of A-10s arrived an hour after that and delivered 130 rounds of 30mm into the same target area.[199]

The devastating airpower unleashed on the ravine stopped the last significant chance for the al-Qaeda to reinforce and prolong the battle. "Target neutralized—200 to

300 personnel in the open," a controller reported.[200] It was reported that a Coalition special operations team had ventured into the valley the next morning and described the scene as "unbelievable carnage" with "pink mist still in the air." "I mean to put it bluntly, when you air burst MK-82 against human flesh, it's got an amazing effectiveness," one A-10 pilot said. One of the Predator pilots told him "the next morning they were following a trail of dead up that valley."[201]

The airstrikes had a direct impact on the battle. TF *Rakkasan* held defensive positions above BPs *Lisa*, *Amy*, *Cindy* and *Diane* by the evening of 5 March 2002. Al-Qaeda reinforcements, ravaged by airpower, were powerless to stop them. The next day, 6 March 2002, a U.S. Army Infantry Battalion completed its pass through the lines of another conventional unit and held BPs *Diane* and *Eve*, thereby "dominating Objective *Ginger* with observation, direct and indirect fires." TF *Summit* was now in position to attack *Ginger* on order. TF *Rakkasan* as a whole continued armed reconnaissance patrols to search out resistance.[202]

The air component kept up its strikes. For example, on 6 March, a B-52 dropped WCMD CBU-103s on immediate request targets at 0545 local time and released a string of MK-82s on the Whale fifteen minutes later.[203] That night, a USAF SOF controller who was already in the area with the brigade TAC directed AC-130 gunship fire several times. He directed a second gunship to attack al-Qaeda and supply caches along the Rat Line. This kind of rapid, precise and persistent engagement from the air helped turn the battle in the TF *Rakkasan's* favor.[204]

Changes in Air Support

The challenge for Operation ANACONDA was to use the ample available strike aircraft in the most efficient way possible. But this was no conventional battlefield with a tried and true architecture for linking up the air and land component. As General Moseley commented:

> It would have been ideal on minute one, night one, to have A-10s, F-15Es, F-16s, F-18s, B-1s, B-52s, U-2 ETP and P-3 AIP [anti-submarine improvement program] and Predators up so that everything was covered...It would have been ideal prior to this first infil to hit those 64 or 65 targets near [sic] simultaneous so that the shock against the opposition would have been immediate, and then to provide suppressing fires prior to the infil, and then supporting fires during the infil, so that you wouldn't be mortared by people from the positions that you could have struck. It would have been ideal to have the comms [communications] up so that the connectivity from CAOC to Bagram, Bagram to CAOC to AWACS, JSTARS, and the fighters would have been clean, as well as having all 30 teams on the ground with the right set of equipage, with the right training and the right understanding so that a JDAM or a GBU-12 could be used regardless of who the team is....[205]

By 5 March 2002, several significant improvements helped smooth out the process.

The CAOC had been in a "solid fight" since 7 October 2001 and as General Moseley put it; this "was not their first rodeo." The main changes for Operation ANACONDA affected forward locations: beefing up the skeleton ASOC cell at Bagram to improve air-ground coordination, and taking other steps to improve airspace management. "What we had was a better understanding and arrangement of activities at Bagram," said General Moseley. "So I would tell you it wasn't the CAOC that got better at this; it was Bagram that got better at this, and cleaned up the misperception and confusion relative to who they could talk to, what systems were up, what was the ROE, etc."[206]

One improvement was the use of strike aircraft as FAC-airborne (FAC-A). During earlier phases of Operation ENDURING FREEDOM, Coalition fighter and attack aircraft often worked as FAC-As, but the rushed air planning for Operation ANACONDA had not provided for this additional control measure. The FAC-As helped overcome the limitations of steep terrain, limited pre-brief information on ground force positions, and the small battlespace. Sometimes it was a full-time job. One pilot from the 332nd Expeditionary Operational Support Squadron said "I went from being the FAC-A that works all the airplanes in on the targets and some strikes myself" to focusing on the deconfliction of aircraft. "I was a big time traffic cop out there," he continued, "just trying to direct people and keep people from running into each other, keeping JDAMs from dropping through people..."[207]

Another improvement was designating engagement zones and pre-planned targets. Based on guidance from CFLCC-Fwd, the CAOC activated three main engagement zones with pre-selected DMPIs. One was on the whale and one was along the southeastern edge of the battle, a ravine known as the Rat Line. Other engagement zones dotted the area and could be opened when friendly ground forces were not present. A USAF lieutenant colonel at the CAOC explained the system during Operation ANACONDA:

> ...the crews carried the entire DMPI list with them (over 3,000 by the end of the operation) If the crews were not tasked to perform XCAS during their vul periods, we [the time-sensitive targeting (TST) cell] would coordinate with the BCD and task out DMPIs during the last 30 minutes or so of their vul. The Army's guidance was to maintain a steady rain of bombs to keep down on the heads of the enemy. We could not task out specific DMPIs before a mission and in the ATO because the ground situation was too fluid and special engagement zones were activated and deactivated at random intervals.[208]

Pre-planned targets allowed XCAS aircraft could drop bombs even when controllers did not have immediate request, or deconfliction stood in the way.

As a result, the number of bombs recorded as "pre-planned XCAS" increased steadily from less than 15 on 2 March 2002, to over 50 on 5 March 2002, and to nearly 100 on 8 March 2002. After 10 March 2002, XCAS strikes on pre-planned DMPIs outnumbered immediate strikes for the rest of Operation ANACONDA.

As the pre-planned XCAS increased, the ASOC and the CAOC were sometimes at odds over prioritization. From the ASOC, the Assistant Division ALO's view was:

> Now everything on the ATO said XCAS, so in my own mind, right or wrong, I thought they belonged to me to push to my ground FACs. The CAOC said 'no, they belong to us'....[209]

From the CAOC's Chief of Combat Operations perspective, "CAS was the priority, but where we can deconflict and continue to do pre-planned strikes into those engagement zones, we're going to do it."[210]

Intricate rules of engagement still caused confusion as the volume and type of air strike taskings mushroomed. Small slices of the battlefield could be opened up for strikes, but when targets fell outside the specially-designated area, they were still subject to the tight rules of Operation ENDURING FREEDOM. General Moseley said:

> If it's outside an engagement zone, because of collateral damage issues and because of infrastructure issues that we lived with since October [2001], the staff at Tampa and the CINC withheld the authority to strike...When you think in terms of other government agencies, Coalition people running around, not knowing about civilians who may or may not be combatants, not knowing about movements of humanitarian entities that were beginning to come into the country...is that a bad or a good Toyota? You have TSTs that are ongoing all the time.

He also explained that even with the focus on the infiltration activities, there were still TSTs and high-value targets to pursue; and phone calls to be made to General Franks and Secretary of Defense Rumsfeld, concerning strike approval for certain targets and the range of civilian, collateral damage and infrastructure issues over which USCENTCOM had held authority all during Operation ENDURING FREEDOM.[211]

There was never any doubt that GFACs had the authority to call in fires. Yet even then, the terrain and the nature of the fight created stops and starts. Small teams were separated, often blocked visually by the terrain, and had to share sensors, radio frequencies, and information in innovative ways. This created two constraints. First, due to the natural ebb and flow of the battle, a typical ground controller might have many targets at one point, and then no targets for hours. Second, deconfliction was essential with 1,400 conventional forces in a small area and with SOF forces woven in, too. The task for Airmen was to keep aircraft available when ground controllers had requests, and to funnel multiple strikes into a tiny ground battle area without causing mid-air collisions.

Most of all, the air component continued to deliver round-the-clock close air support. U.S. Air Force, Navy, and Marine Corps aircrew mission reports (MISREPs) told a very consistent story of close cooperation, repeated efforts to find and strike targets, and strikes that generally satisfied the controllers' requests. Their frustrations included having to break off search or attack efforts and "bingo out" due to fuel state; occasional episodes of not getting clearance due to other aircraft in the area; and spotting targets that for some reason were not approved for strike, generally because of friendlies in the area or TST rules.[212] For example, an AC-130 gunship operating on 7 March 2002 was unable to engage its first targets "due to bomber runs." Later, the gunship's crew spotted possible al-Qaeda supplies near Marzak but could not strike them because of two SOF teams thought to be in the area at unknown locations.[213] As for the controllers, they sometimes worked strike aircraft and had "eyes on" only to have the strikers called away to satisfy another request.

Was the impact of close air support apparent at higher headquarters? Battle reporting suggests that the answer was yes, to a degree. CJTF *Mountain's* reports noted on 7 March 2002 that "CJTF *Mountain* continued to interdict the southeast Rat Line IVO [in vicinity of] Objective *Ginger* and the southern Rat Line with B-52 and AC-130 strikes."[214] Still, it was difficult to say how much of the cumulative success of the airstrikes (as well as the periodic failures) made it back to headquarters as a coherent picture. At this stage of the battle, the aggregate information simply was not available, especially given the limited ASOC cell in place at Bagram. The best assessment of the impact of close air support during the battle came from the nightly CJTF *Mountain* reports to CFLCC. "Due to increased bombing and CAS the enemy was unable to sustain any effective fires upon our forces," stated CJTF *Mountain's* evening report on 7 March 2002. "The al-Qaeda/Taliban fighters appear to be in disarray," observed CJTF *Mountain*. "They have failed to achieve any significant amount of observed fire within the past 24 hours." [215]

Seizing Objective *Ginger*

The final phase of Operation ANACONDA consisted of two tasks: taking Objective *Ginger* and clearing the whale so that Afghan military forces could move into the Shahi Kot valley.

CJTF *Mountain's* outlook was determined but cautious. Small groups of enemy were still moving around Objective *Ginger*. "Each group, if patient, still poses a significant threat to our ground forces and helos," stated CJTF *Mountain*. This was accompanied by the highest estimate of resistance: 600-700 personnel on 2 March 2002, reinforced by "100-200 from the surrounding area." CJTF *Mountain* expected troops to receive sporadic mortar, RPG, and small arms fire.[216]

The more accurate estimates of enemy strength were taken into account in gearing up to bring combat operations to a close. Word of the revised estimates also reached Washington. As CJCS General Myers told CNN on 10 March 2002: "before we went in there, we heard everywhere from 200 to several thousand. We think there were hundreds. And what's left, we think, is a small part of that, but it's still going to take some time to figure that out." [217]

Bad weather closed in just as conventional forces got into place to attack. By 1300 local time on 7 March 2002, ceilings had dropped to 20,000 feet MSL, a level far too low for the mountain peaks in the area. Operations paused. Conventional forces asked for more supplies to hold out through the inclement late-winter weather. AC-130 gunships working on the night of 8 March 2002 were occasionally unable to see areas tasked by controllers due to weather.[218] Still, the tasking was for CJTF *Mountain* to "aggressively stop the infiltration and exfiltration of AQ [al-Qaeda] and Taliban forces along the Rat Lines through use of CAS."[219]

Air attacks kept up the pressure. JDAMs were impervious to weather. From 8 March 2002 onwards, aircraft delivered more than a hundred bombs a day—mostly GBU-31 JDAMs and MK-82s—on the "pre-planned" targets in areas selected by the CFLCC. For example, a pair of F/A-18Cs dropped two JDAMs on a communications facility on 8 March 2002. [220]

Aircrews also used other innovative techniques to search out the remaining al-Qaeda and Taliban. In the early morning hours of 8 March 2002, two A-10s (now flying night missions only from Jacobabad) were "perched" above an AC-130 gunship. With gunships always in the area at night, too, they formed a tactical partnership as the A-10s started taking advantage of the sensors on the gunships. On this night the gunship was attacking troops and gun emplacements on a hillside east of the Rat Lines. The A-10s followed the gunship's direction to strafe a covered vehicle at 0214 local time, and then put six MK-82 airbursts on the hillside at 0243 local time.[221]

At 0407 and 0416 local times 2 F-15Es placed a total of 12 airburst MK-82s on troops in the open. B-1s with JDAM and B-52s with a mix of JDAMs and MK-82s attacked from 0515 to 0629 local time. From 0800 to 0835 local time, a pair of F-16CGs released 8 GBU-12s, then finished up with two strafing passes delivering 250 rounds each. Four Marine Corps AH-1 Cobras attacked cave sites on the west side of the whale at 1400 local time on 8 March 2002.

The culminating attack on Objective *Ginger* was due to begin on 9 March 2002 with another AH-1 Cobra strike on the whale. Early in the morning, at 0641 local time, the strike was cancelled due to poor weather. Official word of the delay of the whole seizure operation came mid-morning at 1027 local time. CJTF *Mountain* planned another weather call at 1500 local time. By then, the weather was cooperating and forces were ready for what would now be a night attack.

This attack looked very different from the operations a week earlier when the teams near Objective *Ginger* had to be extracted. Commanders had multiple eyes on the enemy and beyond doubt expected a fight.

Air support was extensive for the 9 March 2002 operation. More bombs were dropped from fixed-wing aircraft on 9 March (327 total) and 10 March 2002 (340 total) than on any other days of Operation ANACONDA. The sun set at 1731 local time. Fifteen minutes later, AH-1 Cobras (taking advantage of better weather at Bagram) arrived to destroy mortar positions on the southern tip of the whale. Attack helicopters, fighters, bombers, and gunships delivered a persistent, lethal barrage for 75 minutes from 1745 until 1900 local time.

- 1700: B-52 attacks Rat Line

- 1745-1803: F/A-18s attack preplanned targets with MK-82s, GBU-12s and GBU-31s as "prep fires IVO *Ginger*"

- 1745: AH-1s attack the whale

- 1845: B-52 neutralizes Rat Line

- 1830: B-1 release JDAMs on immediate request targets

- 1850: Two AH-64s destroy enemy IVO Objective *Ginger*

- 1900: Two A-10s destroy enemy IVO Objective *Ginger*

While the A-10s finished their attack run, conventional forces commenced their attack on Objective *Ginger* at 1957 local time. It was secured eight hours later at 0405 local time on the morning of 10 March 2002. The next morning, at 0930 local time, troops at *Ginger* took sniper fire. They called in an F-16C for CAS to suppress it.[222]

Afghan Forces Clear the Whale

Meanwhile, the *Hammer* in the original hammer and anvil plan had been significantly strengthened. Afghan forces once again occupied the little whale, also known as Objective *Payback*, during the late afternoon of 8 March 2002 (See Figure 5).

Figure 5: Objective *Payback* or the Little Whale

An additional 700 Afghan forces lined up to occupy the whale. On 11 March 2002, the CFLCC's SITREP stated that CJTF *Mountain* was setting the conditions to clear the whale. That afternoon, Afghan forces positioned two T-55s and six BMPs near the whale and began moving some of his infantry. By 1945 local time that evening, the Commander had established his command post and mortar positions. The other Commander secured the southern pass the next morning and occupied Babulkyel. Forces moved over the whale and down the eastward slope into Serhkhankel at 0940 local time on 12 March 2002, while his tanks and additional forces attacked toward Serhkhankel. The two forces continued clearing the Shahi Kot valley and began to link up at 1023 local time that morning. Twelve vehicles with troops went on to Marzak.[223]

Air support remained constant during this phase of the operation and efficiency improved. A four-ship of F/A-18s launched from USS *John C. Stennis* at 1500 local time and held over Objective *Remington*. One F/A-18 had to return to the ship with radio problems, but JSTARS efficiently directed the other three to release a combination of precision and non-precision weapons on targets in the Shahi Kot valley over a 25-minute period as dusk fell. One F/A-18 delivered a GBU-12 at 1735 local time. Another dropped GBU-12s at 1352 local time and made a second pass, this time at a 15 degree dive angle, to deliver two MK-82s at 1800 local time. The fourth recorded drops of GBU-12s at 1752 and made a dive-bomb pass with MK-82s one minute later at 1753 local time. JSTARS assessed "all hits were good" for this mission.[224]

That same day, the Marine Corps AH-1 Cobras again provided support with a jump FARP. According to a report by the 13th Marine Expeditionary Unit:

> On 11 March [2002] during Operation HARPOON, CTF-*165* initially used 2xCH-53E to refuel the Cobras. When they were nearly drained, a CH-47D came in to replace them in the FARP role. The CH-53Es climbed up and conducted HAR [helicopter aerial refueling] with USMC KC-130s, then returned to the jump FARP to replace the CH-47D.[225]

The jump FARP kept the Cobras operating for several hours consecutively.

Conventional forces had already moved out of the area as the Afghan forces linked up to complete exploitation of the Shahi Kowt valley. Reports during the battle commented on likely exfiltration by small numbers of al-Qaeda. Those who slipped past the Operation ANACONDA cordon might find little to bar their way to Pakistan. But for the most part, the seizure of all desired blocking positions sealed off escape routes.

As late as 16 March 2002, CJTF *Mountain* reported that there was a "high level of vehicular activity in the eastern portions of the mountains west of Khowst valley," the slopes where the 10th Mountain Division had fought to hold its positions. However, the vehicles could not be identified as hostile or friendly.[226]

By then, the second mission of Operation ANACONDA was in full swing. Cave and other exploitation teams in Operation HARPOON were combing the whale, Marzak, and other locations. Before dawn on 14 March 2002 a unit of Coalition conventional light ground forces was inserted to help with the operation. At around 0900 local time immediate close air support was requested. Fifteen minutes later, after the airstrike, they reported two enemy KIA and continued their cave exploitation.[227] Ultimately over 30 caves on the whale were exploited.[228]

Activity in Operation ANACONDA tapered off after 14 March 2002. Two days later, CJTF *Mountain* was able to report to CFLCC that there were less than 15 enemy personnel in the "entire ANACONDA area." SOF Teams remained in place watching the ridgeline. Other coalition, Afghan, and Special Forces worked in teams to complete sensitive site exploitation. But the battle was over. At Objective *Remington*, the whale, and Objective *Glock* (in the southeast) the report continued:

> …no enemy contact has been reported in the last 48 hours, with the only exception being a SOF team encountering four personnel on 15 March 2002 as they attempted to flee from the whale. We assess the few potential enemy remaining in the area will only present themselves if they fear capture or death from Coalition forces on the ground approaching their hide locations….the true enemy threat no longer exists.[229]

With this assessment, Operation ANACONDA came to a close. "Thank goodness for the bravery of those soldiers that we were able to take the fight to the enemy and be successful here," said General Myers.[230]

Chapter Six

Persistent Close Air Support

CJTF *Mountain*'s daily reports to the CFLCC at Camp Doha attested over and over again to the value of airpower in Operation ANACONDA. Anecdotes and after-action reports from ground controllers who called in the strikes confirmed that close air support was generally effective and frequently devastating.

When CJTF *Mountain* projected that "the CJTF will continue to use fires to isolate objective area and destroy the enemy" the primary fires tool available was coalition close air support.[231]

However, the view from Bagram of air support during Operation ANACONDA was not—and could not be—complete. The full statistical picture emerged only months later in analysis of sorties flown and bombs dropped. Figure 6 shows the number of strike sorties flown for Operation ANACONDA.

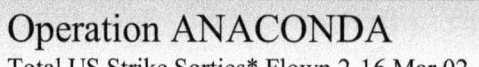
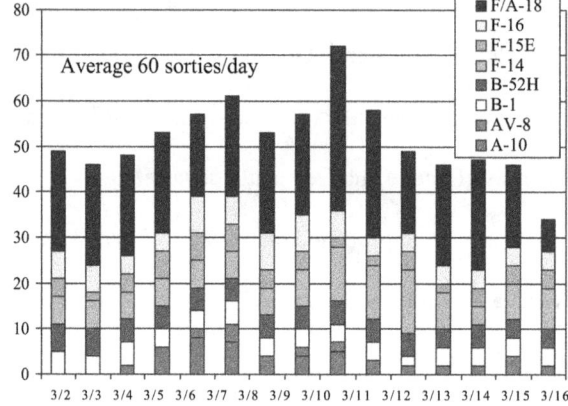

Figure 6: Operation ANACONDA Strike Sorties Flown

After the battle, analysis of the aggregate data showed that the air component pulled off a tremendous achievement in concentrating precision firepower and mass into a very small area. General Moseley said "this is a really small piece of sky" and "we were pushing a lot of things in there, manned and unmanned, and we were dropping a lot of things through it."[232]

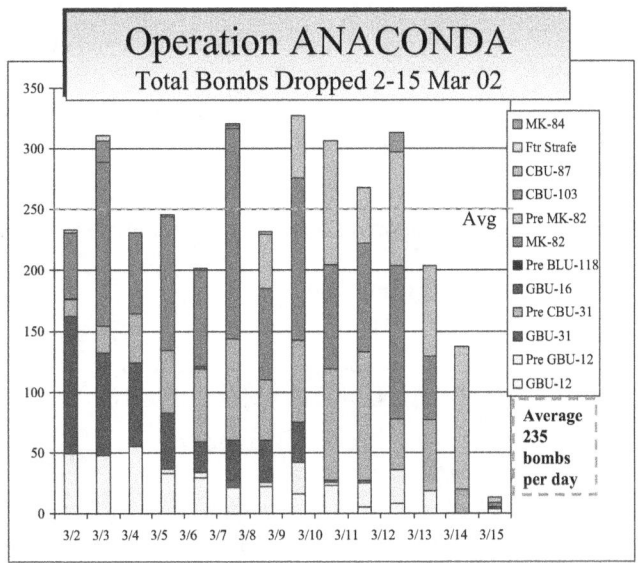

Figure 7: Operation ANACONDA Total Bombs Dropped, 2-15 Mar 2002

The aggregate data compiled give a much clearer picture of the effectiveness of air support. While the number of sorties flown documents the steady XCAS provided, another important measure of effectiveness was the number of bombs dropped in the Operation ANACONDA battle area. These were tracked in a division fire support coordination element (DFSCOORD) database that registered full information on the strikes, down to the target coordinates, type of weapon dropped, platform, target description, and so on. Covering the period from 2 – 15 March 2002, it provides information on just over 3,500 weapons released. All statistics on weapons dropped as depicted in charts or cited in this section were compiled from analysis of that database.

Precision ordnance (mainly GBU-12s and JDAMs) was used along with a quantity of MK-82 weapons, often set for airburst to attack troops and firing positions. The B-52s dropped the lion's share of the MK-82s (over 1,600) but several other types of aircraft from A-10s to F/A-18s to F-15Es also employed the MK-82, because it was a preferred munition for attacking targets like troops in the open and mortar firing positions. The division of 47 percent precision and 53 percent non-precision ordnance is depicted in the chart.

Persistence was another important metric. Strikes took place day and night in response to calls from forward air controllers.

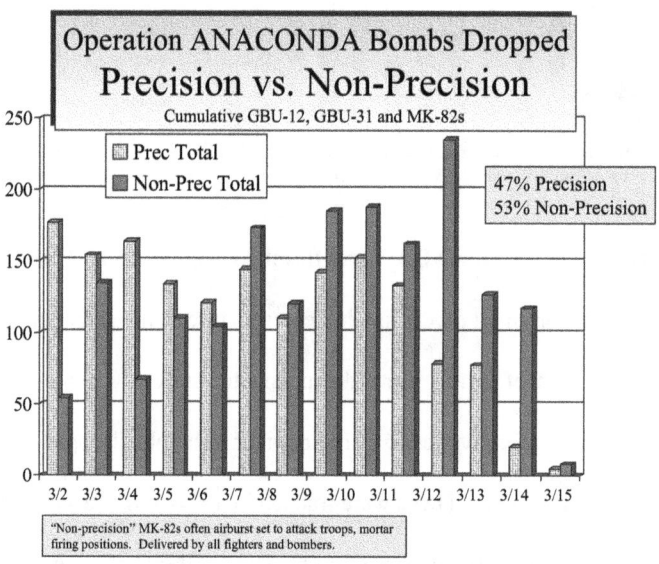

Figure 8: Operation ANACONDA Munitions Used

Another important shift was the addition of "pre-planned" strikes on areas selected by the CFLCC. This helped to manage the flow of airstrikes into the battlespace. While all strikes were grouped as XCAS—airborne close air support—they were divided into "immediate" strikes on targets called in, passed, or talked on by controllers; and pre-planned strikes based on DMPIs in the immediate area selected by CFLCC-Fwd and processed by the CAOC. For the first week, immediate XCAS strikes outnumbered strikes on preplanned targets. But by 9 March 2002, the balance had shifted.

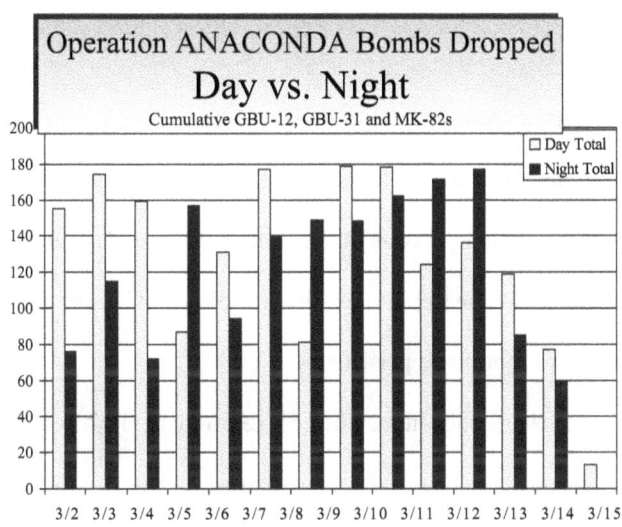

Figure 9: Operation ANACONDA Bombs Dropped

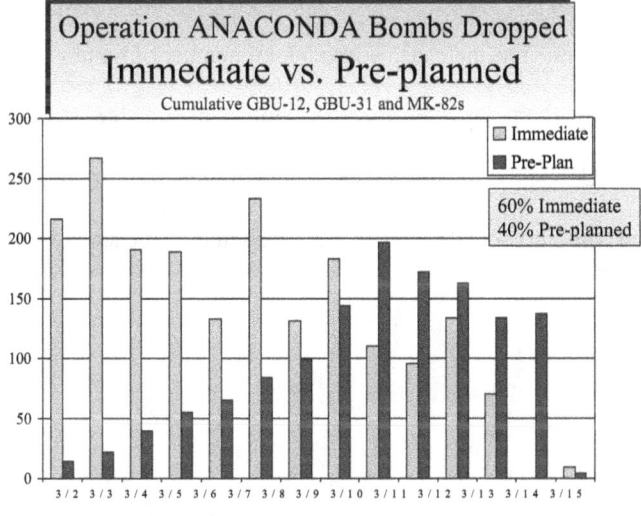

Figure 10: Operation ANACONDA CAS Sorties by Category

The increase in pre-planned targets reflected diminishing numbers of requests from ground controllers and a greater ability to use a fighter or bomber's ordnance at the end of its vulnerability period, instead of sending the aircrew home to record a no-drop.

Hour-by-Hour Airstrike Analysis

While the aggregate statistics for each day show the level and nature of the effort, those in the heat of the battle worked in minutes and hours, not days and weeks.

Taking the analysis one step further, the breakdown of bombs dropped by hour confirms that close air support was persistent.

The following charts show three different sets of data. First is a graph with the number of bombs dropped per hour. The times are recorded in ZULU time. However, the light blue box identifies daylight hours for the Afghanistan Theater. To the right, a small graph totals up the number of precision vs. non-precision weapons for the day depicted. On the bottom is a spreadsheet repeating the numbers used to form the graph for that day's airstrikes. The table also adds up total number of bombs dropped by type; by day; and by night. (Note: on a few days, the table depicts fighter strafes and expenditure of GBU-16s. However, as these were minimal, they are not depicted in the graph. Also, the tables do not tally cluster munitions in the precision or non-precision categories.)

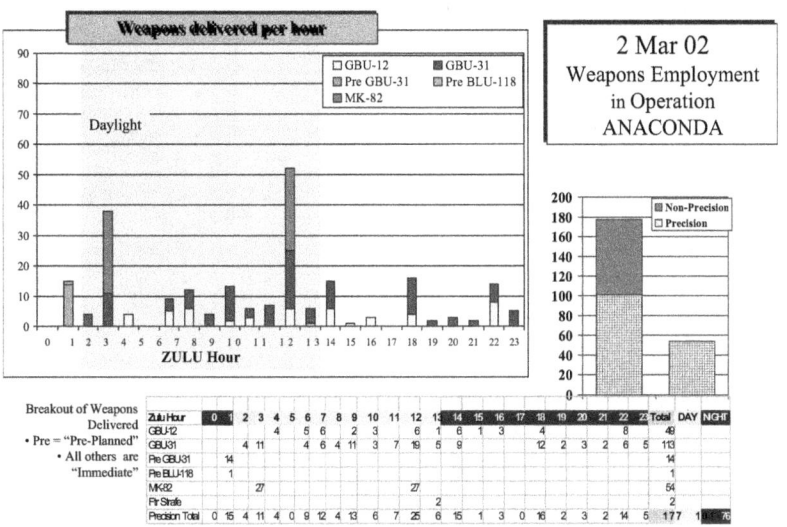

Figure 11: 2 March 2003 Weapons Employment

On 2 March 2002, for example, 231 bombs were dropped. The first several days of the conflict also saw several occasions when fighters were asked to strafe. Strafing began with two F/A-18Cs on the first day. It was not uncommon for controllers to request a fighter strafe, *then* task the same aircraft to expend its bombs.

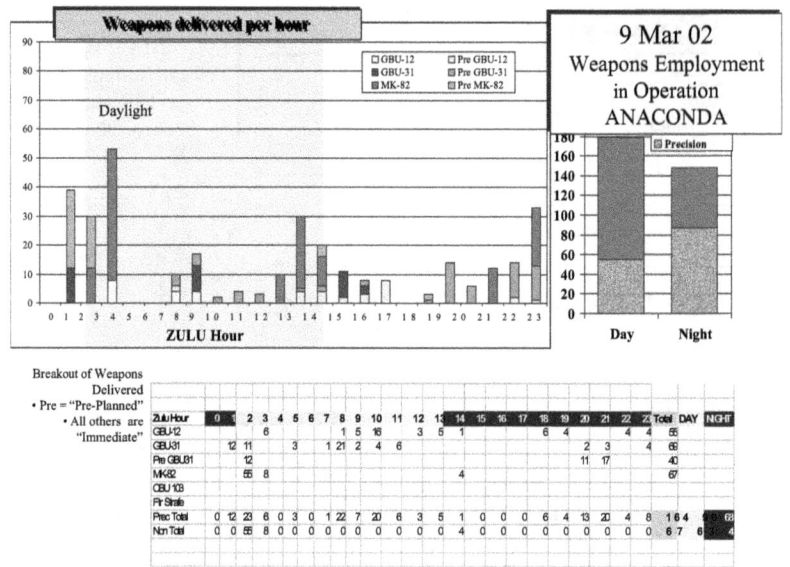

Figure 12: 9 March 2002 Weapons Employment

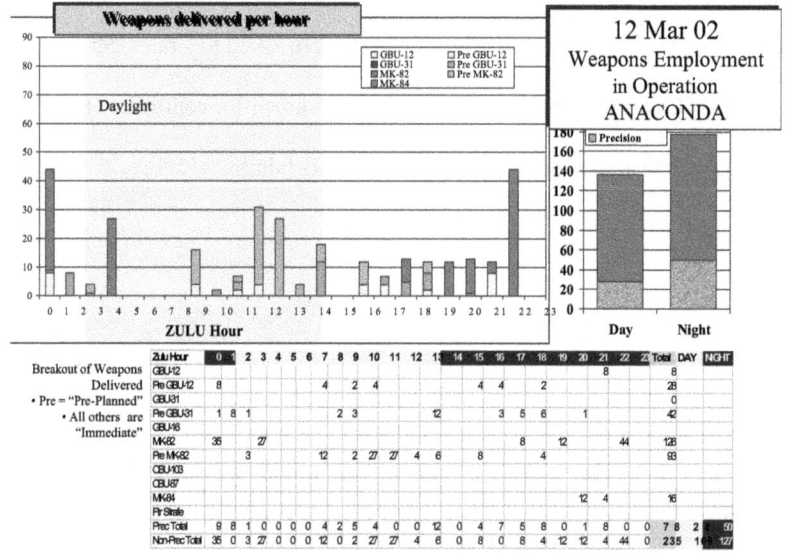

Figure 13: 12 March 2002 Weapons Employment

The two heaviest days of ordnance expenditure came on 9 and 10 March 2002 as the conventional forces were gearing up for and launching the successful attack to take Objective *Ginger*. On 9 March 2002, 327 bombs were dropped, and on 10 March 2002, the number was 340. Both days saw a higher expenditure of non-precision munitions—the MK-82s—than precision munitions. Day and night strikes were nearly even. The only major difference on these two days was that while the number of immediate bombs dropped was somewhat greater on 9 March 2002, the number of pre-planned strikes was significantly higher than immediate ones on 10 March 2002.

As General Corley stated: "There was not a place or space on that battlefield that we could not have rained down kinetic kill ammunition. Period."[233]

Consistent coverage was one indicator that the airstrikes were responsive to the fire support requirements of those on the ground. However, many factors influenced the timeliness of strikes. Deconflicting airstrikes was a difficult job for the fire support element and the small ASOC cell that assisted it. Over 200 fire support coordinating measures (FSCM) were in place—some permissive, some restrictive.

The fire support element and ASOC cell at Bagram were so busy during Operation ANACONDA and so limited in their communications and equipment that it was impossible to generate an aggregate picture of what the airstrikes were or were not accomplishing. General Hagenbeck, CJTF *Mountain*, later commented:

> By the time the AWACS handed a target off, the Air Force said it took 26 minutes to calculate the DMPI, which is required to ensure the precision munition hits the target. Then the aircraft had to get into the airspace management queue. It took anywhere from 26 minutes to hours (on occasion) for the precision munitions to hit the targets.[234]

However, the data point of 26 minutes was cited inaccurately. The number was actually an average response time that came from a study of data provided by some of the

GFACs who called in airstrikes during Operation ANACONDA. Only 34 incidents had both the request time and the tasking time available.

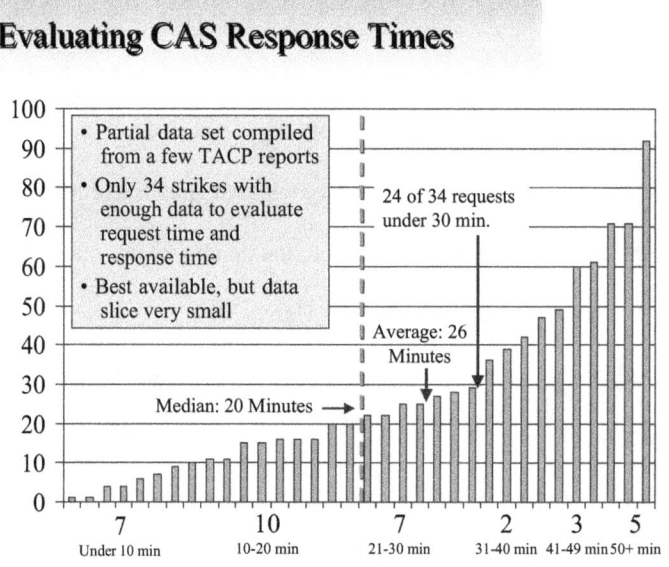

Figure 14: Close air support response timing[235]

The fact remains that the data set is very small and, therefore, probably does not fully represent statistics from which to generalize. For example, on 4 March 2002, one GFAC, the one nearest the Roberts Ridge crash site, is listed with just one request in the mid-afternoon, filled by a B-1 crew in only six minutes. Logs record many other strikes, such as the strafing F-15Es, delivered to that area. The GFAC himself recalled making about 30 requests that day. For this reason, the data set used to evaluate response times is both incomplete and too small for a definitive conclusion.

A preliminary USCENTCOM report put it succinctly: "Although the airpower resource always exceeded the claimant's requirement, the stovepipe nature of the command and control system put the claimants in competition for these available resources, sometimes during execution, and placed strains on the ACE's ability to distribute fires in accordance with the CJTF *Mountain* commander's guidance."

However, the report continued: "Despite the in-execution leap in requirements for airstrikes, CAS was responsive and pivotal to the ultimate success. All requests were met, according to air request documentation and feedback from GFACs, FSEs, aircrew, ACC, and CAOC personnel."[236]

Chapter Seven

Observations

On 16 March 2002, CJTF *Mountain* reported that Operation ANACONDA was complete.

> CJTF *Mountain* forces successfully accomplished the key tasks of denying the enemy a base of operation in the lower Shahi Kot valley, killed or captured a significant number of the known remaining hard core aq [Al Qaeda] fighters and exploited the objective area for future use to prevent future terrorist activities. CJTF *Mountain* successfully massed overwhelming combat power and destroyed a well-organized and tenacious enemy.[237]

This operational summary spoke volumes about how different the outcome of Operation ANACONDA was from the original plan set in motion two weeks earlier. The operation had taken several days longer, tasked coalition forces heavily, and required more support of all kinds—from CAS to commitment of the reserve—than anticipated.

Yet it had worked. In Washington, General Pace said: "The enemy forces that were there, to the best of our knowledge, are not there now."[238]

After the casualties at the very start of the operation, there were no friendly fire deaths, and no fatalities among the conventional ground forces. It was a tribute to tactical excellence and leadership on the ground; and to hard work and discipline in the air. "How, in an 8 by 8 square mile area, that we had 42 ETACs, roughly 1,500 friendlies and 800 to 1,000 enemy, that we did not kill a friendly, I have no idea to this day," commented one USAF lieutenant colonel. "I second that, I have no idea," added a USAF major who was at Bagram.[239] However, at the time of this comment, individuals were unaware of the friendly fire event on Day 1 as the final friendly fire report was not completed for several months after Operation ANACONDA.[240]

Operation ANACONDA's greatest tragedy was the death of eight Americans killed in action. On the other hand, many more in harm's way not only survived, but also accomplished their mission. By 16 March 2002, the total losses to U.S. forces were eight killed in action (KIA) and 80 wounded in action (WIA), 35 of those wounded were later returned to duty. Afghan military forces lost three KIA—all on the first day—and 30 wounded in action. That brought the total friendly casualties to 11 KIA and 75 WIA.[241] CJTF *Mountain's* 1,411 conventional forces engaged in the battle suffered no combat deaths.

On the ground, CJTF *Mountain's* forces proved their tenacity and ability to adapt quickly. Positions were juggled and reconsolidated when necessary, well-timed extractions conserved friendly strength, and the renewal of the attack and seizure of Objective *Ginger* accomplished the mission's goals. The major achievement was the rapid reworking of operations to take on five times more enemy forces than expected. The U.S. Army Forces Central Command (USARCENT) daily SITREP for 16 March 2002 recorded the revised estimate of enemy forces at 1,000—a number that first appeared on 5 March 2002.[242]

Air support set a new standard. Perhaps never before had Coalition aircraft delivered more precision weapons into such a small area all deemed to be "short of the FSCL." The intensity of strikes in Operation ANACONDA's battlespace surpassed that of Operation DESERT STORM a decade earlier. On 25 February 1991 (the first day for the ground war, Day 39 for the air war) Coalition aircraft flew 140 strike sorties (both interdiction and CAS) against the armored Republican Guard's Tawakalna Division and 12th Armored Division in Killbox AE6. This was the single highest number of airstrikes against any killbox during the ground war.

Another striking statistic was the number of al-Qaeda casualties. The 15 March 2002 CFLCC situation report put the number of assessed al-Qaeda personnel at 1,000. Of these, the SITREP claimed 813 KIA, the sum of 525 confirmed and 288 probable.[243] Operation ANACONDA accomplished its goal of destroying the last significant concentration of al-Qaeda and Taliban conducting coordinated operations inside Afghanistan.

Some Implications

Operation ANACONDA was full of lessons—good and bad—for many aspects of the art of Joint warfare. It was not the intent of this report to go too far beyond what happened or to compete with other, ongoing lessons learned work. Nevertheless, some implications are listed below.

Training

Training and Adaptation. Operation ANACONDA attested to the high-quality training of soldiers, sailors, Marines, and Airmen involved in the fight. Once the execution phase began, soldiers adapted to changing conditions. High physical fitness standards, marksmanship, and small-unit tactics meant the American force on the ground was both better prepared and far better led at the tactical level than their al-Qaeda and Taliban opponents. To be sure, some of the al-Qaeda fighters were well-prepared and well-equipped themselves. General Corley commented:

> Ultimately what we discovered in that objective area was we had some individuals outfitted with Garmin GPS, Northface tents, and parkas. They were well-positioned and had scouted out good positions. They had probably learned some lessons from previous conflicts.[244]

However, even as air assault teams came under immediate, continuous and heavy fire, they adapted rapidly to the battle and executed sound tactical decisions that minimized casualties and contributed to later success. The decision to extract the teams from highly defended areas on the first day and to commit the reserve force on the second day were examples of rapid adaptation by the ground forces.

Similarly, Coalition Airmen pulled off tremendous feats of rapid adaptation. They strafed, bombed, and loitered where necessary to deliver close air support in an area less than a fourth the size of one *Desert Storm*-era kill box. Superb aircrew training paid off in the ability to adapt to unfamiliar missions and do CAS with platforms never designed for that role.

Individual initiative again played a vital role in combat success in coalition support to each other. From a Coalition special operations team that decided to move closer "go help the Americans" to the handful of officers and enlisted ASOC personnel who cobbled together their system and made it work, initiative led to results.

Planning and Preparation

Enemy Situation Estimate. As the CJTF *Mountain* and USARCENT daily reports acknowledged, the 2 March 2002 estimate of enemy forces in the Shahi Kot area was significantly underestimated. Instead of 125-200 enemy, about 1,000 were later estimated to have been in place or within easy reach for reinforcement. Documentary evidence suggests that three factors may have particularly contributed to the low estimate. First, early, higher estimates from December 2001 and January 2002 were based on sources often discarded as unreliable. Second, discussion of the numbers of al-Qaeda and Taliban initially were for the whole Khowst-Gardez area, but the OPORD gave an estimate just for Shahi Kot valley. Third, CFLCC-Fwd intelligence (the ACE, or Analysis and Control Element) functioned at about one-third the manning level when it arrived at Karshi-Khanabad compared to 70 when the ACE was on its Kosovo Force (KFOR) rotation.)[245]

Late Notification to the Air Component for Planning. Insufficient coordination between the land and air components at all levels was also a problem. Operation ANACONDA was planned in the first half of February 2002, but the air component did not bring its full planning resources to bear until the last week of that month. As CFACC General Moseley put it: "if you exclude a component from the planning and you exclude a component that will provide the preponderance of support, logistic and kinetic, then you will have to live with the outcome of this not playing out very well."[246] Much of the problem seemed to stem from the lack of clear and frequent contact between the right elements of the staffs of the two components. For example, CFLCC General Mikolashek asked about air component involvement as soon as he was briefed on the plan on 17 February 2002, but working-level contacts did not happen for three more days. Tardy notification to the air component affected fire support planning and execution, and made it a challenge to fulfill airlift requirements for combat forces. As General Moseley later told General Franks: "We shouldn't go into this thinking that the air component's going to come in like the cavalry and bail everybody out. We should have all of this happen at the beginning." "Well, if we had it to do all over again, we would," General Franks replied to General Moseley.[247]

Theater Air Control System. As the CFLCC Perspective paper put it: "If we had it to do over again, there would be a significantly increased capability in the Fire Support Element and Air Support Operations Center." While those personnel "rose to the fight that evolved after first contact," the rushed planning for the operation left them long on ingenuity but short on resources.[248] The air support system in Afghanistan prior to Operation ANACONDA was unusual but it met mission requirements during Operation ENDURING FREEDOM's first months. However, those planning Operation ANACONDA failed to see that if stressed, the air request system had weaknesses—lack of visibility, lack of prioritization, lack of suitable and robust communications, etc.—that could cause conflict and make it inefficient in surge close air support operations. The failure to see that the air request system would be stressed was part of the larger failure to anticipate that Operation ANACONDA could turn into an opposed operation. That in turn was based on the OPORD estimation that enemy fighters in the Shahi Kot valley would be few in number and would not put up much resistance.

Limited Airstrikes before H-Hour. The air component also regretted having no opportunity to conduct major preparatory strikes. "It would have been ideal prior to this first infil to hit those 64 or 65 targets nearly simultaneously so that the shock against the opposition would have been immediate, and then to provide suppressing fires prior to the infil, and then supporting fires during the infil, so that you wouldn't be mortared by people from the positions that you could have struck," General Moseley commented.[249]

Shift in Type of Operations. Above all, Operation ANACONDA began without a shift in the mindset for operations in theater. Previous operations had not made the limitations

115

clear. Special operations forces relied on well-equipped controllers to bring in CAS and ground-controlled interdiction strikes a few at a time. The U.S. Marines at Kandahar faced opposition but brought their own air control net. When regular U. S. Army forces prepared for Operation ANACONDA, the deficiencies in ground communications and air control had not been fully exposed and remedied.

Execution

The execution of Operation ANACONDA called on all concerned to deliver maximum effort and to regroup and alter command and control processes during the battle. Ultimately, the operation was successful and loss of life was kept to a minimum. For these reasons, it must be said that the execution of Operation ANACONDA was very good—and at times, heroic and remarkable.

That said, frustration accompanied nearly every aspect of Operation ANACONDA. It must have been disconcerting indeed for ground forces who landed on top of strong enemy resistance to have the initial plan fall apart. However, in the joint context, the main frustration stemmed largely from constraints of various types that appeared to get in the way of delivering air support.

Strike Aircraft Not Employed. As the story of the B-52 during the battle at Takur Gar showed, the major frustrations of air employment often arose over deconfliction. All strike aircraft flew extremely long sorties to get into theater; in many cases, their bombs were not used. The ATO for 3 March 2002 listed 27 of 66 planned strike sorties as dropping ordnance.[287] A review of U.S. Navy mission reports during Operation

ANACONDA shows numerous pilots recording "did not drop" during all phases of the operation. While this was aggravating to aircrews, it illustrated that plenty of air support was available

ASOC Custody of XCAS. Deconfliction was also a problem higher in the chain of command. Both the ASOC at Bagram and the CAOC felt they had authority over sorties labeled XCAS on the ATO. Here, the decision not to apportion sorties to CAS or TST or even the contested term *battlefield air interdiction (BAI)*, as might have been done in a more conventional conflict, led to tussles over ownership. The CAOC and the ASOC often had different perspectives. As the 20ASOS Commander said, "These interdiction missions fell back into the easy box that we were used to in the Air Force."[250] Matters came to a head when the priority was troops-in-contact vs. high value targets. The ASOC was also under-manned and under-equipped, prompting the CFACC to send more personnel to help early in Operation ANACONDA.

Assessment of Air Support Impact. Pilot mission reports, ground controllers reports, and aggregate statistics on sorties flown and munitions expended now paint a picture of persistent, effective and sometimes devastating air support. However, little if any of this integrated perspective was available to headquarters at Bagram during the operation. As a result, dramatic "failures" of airpower—such as the fruitless effort to hit a truck on 2 March 2002—may have colored perceptions.

Command

Component Commanders in Joint Operations. Both the CFLCC and the CFACC were somewhat dissatisfied with their level of insight into the initial planning for Operation ANACONDA. General Moseley said that OPSEC and "maintaining organic capability" made the system less open. "Had the system been more open, and had it in fact offered those things that, as a joint commander, I expected to get before a joint operation, things would have been a whole lot cleaner."[251] What was lacking was a free and full exchange of information about upcoming operations. This can be attributed in part to culture – the land component's general expectation of being "supported" – and in part to the unique rules of the Afghan theater. The tale of the Bagram ASOC cell was an example of the gray areas. While collocated with the CFLCC-Fwd, its senior personnel actually reported to the CFACC. The ASOC function was neglected until the last minute. The land component was preoccupied with its battle rhythm and rehearsals, while the air component worked to build the air plan. Working hard on their pieces of the battle, there was little component initiative to reach out to the other to enhance coordination and effectiveness.

This raises the question of whether the combatant commander—or the component commanders themselves—could or should have forced closer ties. The ties might be "flat" from component to component, or top-down. Either way, as General Moseley put it, "the silver bullet for ANACONDA is better orchestration at the component level."[252]

Conclusion

Operation ANACONDA was successful because the basic idea behind the plan - creating a noose around the Taliban and al-Qaeda hold-outs—was sound and most of all, because of the outstanding tactical leadership and decisions made on the ground and in the air. This was a case of superior performance from soldiers, Special Forces, and Airmen overriding the shortcomings of prior planning and the serious failures of communication between the components. A more robust ASOC could perhaps have lessened the air support frustrations of Operation ANACONDA; but the trials of the ASOC cell were, as General Moseley said, a symptom of the much larger problem of component coordination.

The plan for Operation ANACONDA underestimated two things: first, the enemy situation and its tenacity; and, second, the difficulty of combining conventional and Special Forces operations in the terrain of the Shahi Kot valley area. On the latter point, the use of a 1,500-man air assault force to seize the higher slopes framing the valley marked a major change in the Operation ENDURING FREEDOM conduct of operations. It changed the nature of the war—but the air and land component forces scrambled at the last minute to put proper battlespace command and control procedures and communications into place. Despite this, the desired level of integration was not achieved in time, and it took the first several days of Operation ANACONDA to make air and ground work together to their full capacity as a team.

Inaccurate estimate of the enemy situation—numbers present, reinforcements nearby, and intentions—was perhaps the single major shortfall and it colored the entire operation. Reconstructing the chain of events leading to the OPORD's conclusions sheds some light on why the estimate turned out the way it did. But the fact remains that commanders in every war generally have to make the decision to execute without perfect intelligence. As General Franks said later, "We'll never have the precise picture of any particular place where we're conducting an operation." He also said that "each time we put people in one of these assault helicopters" to move into battle "we all recognize that we're subject to come under immediate attack…"[253] Here again is another reason to build up strong component relationships capable of withstanding the inevitable errors in predicting the enemy's behavior.

The real shortfall was in planning between the air and land components. "The challenge is to open the aperture on this so that more people are involved in a process like this, so that the right sets of questions can be asked earlier, and the pre-positioning and the prep tasks can be done prior to execution," said General Moseley.[254]

Enduring Impact

Operation ANACONDA had an impact well beyond its immediate effect on Operation ENDURING FREEDOM. U.S. Army and U.S. Air Force senior leaders met on 7 November 2002 to discuss issues raised by Operation ANACONDA. Army and Air Force four-stars held their annual warfighter talks 9 – 10 December 2002, and Operation ANACONDA was a major topic of discussion. Improvements to CAS were also major discussion issues in internal Air Force settings (such as the thrice-yearly CORONA four-star conferences and a December 2002 doctrine summit.) The AF/XO staff tracked funding for a range of CAS improvements.

The experiences of 2 – 16 March 2002, also reminded warfighters that CAS remains a complex art best practiced with a full control structure in place. Prior to Operation IRAQI FREEDOM, which began a year later, the CAOC added a fully-staffed CAS cell and made numerous other changes in close air support arrangements. More attention was paid to liaison between the air and land components; to involving all components in early planning; and to setting up theater air control structures tailored to serve the full range of "air support" from interdiction to CAS in many forms.

For General Moseley, who remained as the CFACC for Operation IRAQI FREEDOM a year later, Operation ANACONDA turned out to be valuable preparation for that larger operation. During Operation ANACONDA, "it became obvious" to General Moseley that if the CFLCC had a trusted air liaison officer with him at his headquarters, "that guy could have worked out a lot of this so that the component commanders could have had a lot better visibility on this," General Moseley later said. General Moseley got permission from General Franks, then from Air Force Chief of Staff General John Jumper, and turned the Air Component Coordinating Element (ACCE) into reality, sending a two-star general to the CFLCC headquarters as the CFACC's personal representative. Other ACCEs – senior O-6s and O-7s – fanned out to other headquarters, like that of Combined Forces Maritime Component Commander (CFMCC) VADM Tim Keating in Bahrain. In this and in other ways, Operation ANACONDA acted like shock therapy that motivated the air and land components, and Special Forces, to tighten up their working relationships.[255]

A USAF Senior Airman, who was a SOF combat control team member, put Operation ANACONDA's value into context based on his personal experience. In the end, "the guy who's seen it and done it may not be able to put it into words but he's smarter and he's a better operator for it. So you have a stronger military because of all this." [256]

PHOTO CREDITS

Page 12: Memorial Service for Eight Servicemen Killed in Operation ANACONDA. Extracted from Slide 41 of 42 in Special Tactics Operations PowerPoint presentation. See, Special Tactics Operations, Battle Of Takur Ghar Ridge, Operation ANACONDA, 3 - 4 March 2002, TFELR. (Secret).

Page 39. U.S. Air Force controller in Operation ANACONDA. Extracted from HQ ACC presentation, "ANACONDA Assertions & Facts (U)," n.d. (Secret//X1, X4).

Page 59: C-17 Globemaster III transports keep the troops at Bagram, Afghanistan, supplied. This one, from McChord Air Force Base, taxis onto a parking spot on the ramp so it can offload cargo and fuel. Afghan trucks deliver the fuel to Army helicopters. Photo by MSgt Keith Reed. Published in *Airman* Magazine, May 2002 Web Edition, The Afghan Air Link, "Keeping Operation ENDURING FREEDOM supplied and on track," by MSgt Louis A. Arana-Barradas.

ENDNOTES

Note: Classification caveat found in the endnote identify the classification of the original source document which may remain classified. The endnotes within this document were reviewed for declassification and determined that they are releasable to the public.

[1] General Tommy R. Franks, Commander, U.S. Central Command, quoted in *Defense Department Special Briefing: Report on the Battle of Takur Ghar,* 24 May 2002, found in Task Force *Enduring Look* Repository, hereafter cited as TFELR.

[2] Anaconda CONOPS Briefing, 20 Feb 2002.

[3] Lt Gen T. Michael Moseley, Operation ENDURING FREEDOM CFACC, "TFEL Interview (U)," 14 January 2003.

[4] Lt Gen T. Michael Moseley, Operation ENDURING FREEDOM CFACC, "TFEL Interview (U)," 14 January 2003. (Secret//X1, X4).

[5] Airstrike impact quoted in CJTF *Mountain* to CFLCC, 032100Z Mar 02.

[6] Report, CJTF *Mountain* to CFLCC, 042100Z 19ASOS, Mar 02.

[7] AFA Magazine, Oct 2002, Vol 85, No 9, *The Airpower of ANACONDA*, article by Rebecca Grant

[8] Details of the operation are found in DoD Briefing, "Background briefing on the Report of the Battle of Takur Ghar," May 24, 2002, official DoD Transcript.

[9] Report, CJTF *Mountain* to CFLCC, (U) 052100Z Mar 02.

[10] (U) GFAC report, Operation ANACONDA After Action Report, (U) 15 March 2002.

[11] Report CJTF *Mountain* to CFLCC, (U) 072100Z Mar 02.

[12] Report CJTF *Mountain* to CFLCC, (U) March 16, 2002.

[13] General Richard B. Myers, USAF, Chairman, Joint Chiefs of Staff, Interview with Wolf Blitzer, CNN, 10 March 2002.

[14] General Tommy Franks, USCENTCOM, "DoD Special Briefing on Takur Gar,"

[15] General Moseley, TFEL Interview (U), 14 January 2003. (Secret//X1, X4).

[16] TF Rakkasan TACP AAR

[17] Two U.S. Air Force, one U.S. Navy, and five U.S. Army personnel lost their lives during Operation ANACONDA. See, Eric Bradley and David Kelly, Times Staff reporters, "8 Men From 3 Services unite in Fight That was Their Last," Los Angeles Times, 6 March 2002, found on-line at http://www.latimes.com/news/nationworld/nation/la-030602soldiers,1,327964.story.

[18] General Tommy R. Franks, Commander, U.S. Central Command, quoted in *Defense Department Special Briefing: Report on the Battle of Takur Ghar,* 24 May 2002, found in Task Force *Enduring Look* Repository, hereafter cited as TFELR.

[19] General Franks, *Report on the Battle of Takur Ghar,* 24 May 2002, TFELR.

[20] Graphic developed by Task Force *Enduring Look.*

[21] Lt Col, USAF, former chief of combat operations at CAOC, "Interview with TFEL (U)," 7 August 2002, TFELR. (Secret//X1, X4).

[22] Graphic developed by Task Force *Enduring Look.*

[23] General Richard B. Myers, USAF, Chairman of Joint Chiefs of Staff, quoted in Interview with Wolf Blitzer (U), CNN, 10 March 2002, TFELR.

[24] General Peter Pace, USMC, Vice Chairman of Joint Chiefs of Staff, quoted in DoD News Briefing, 12 December 2001, TFELR.

[25] Lt Col, USAF, 20ASOS/CC, "Interview with TFEL (U)," 19 August 2002, TFELR. (Secret//X1, X4).

[26] Donald R. Rumsfeld, Secretary of Defense, quoted in DoD News Briefing, 19 December 2001, TFELR.

[27] Graphic developed internally by Task Force Enduring Look.

[28] Operations; Ground Force Operations (U), 1 Jan 2002, TFELR. (Secret//X1, X4).

[29] CJFLCC Operations; Ground Force Operations (U), 1 Jan 2002, TFELR. (Secret//X1, X4).

[30] OPORD 02-21, FRAGO 06 KHOWST-GARDEZ 120001Z JAN 2002 (U). (Secret//X1, X4).

[30] Cited in "Point Paper, Operation ANACONDA, CFLCC Perspective (U)," 16 March 2002, TFELR. (Secret//X1, X4).

[31] Cited in "Point Paper, Operation ANACONDA, CFLCC Perspective (U)," 16 March 2002, TFELR. (Secret//X1, X4).

[32] Lt Col, 20ASOS/CC, "Interview with TFEL (U)," 19 August 2002, TFELR. (Secret//X1, X4).

[33] TF's early plan for Operation ANACONDA is cited in this interview. See Dep 20ASOS/CC, USAF, director of support for 20TASS, "Interview with TFEL (U)," 20 May 2002, TFELR. (Secret//X1, X4).

[34] TFEL Roberts Ridge review (S), Holmes comments, 21 June 2002, TFELR. (Secret//X1, X4).

[35] Point Paper, Operation ANACONDA CFLCC Perspective (U), 16 March 2002, (Secret//X1, X4).

[36] 20 ASOS/CC, "Interview with TFEL (U)," 19 August 2002, TFELR. (Secret//X1, X4).

[37] Observation on value of HUMINT cited in ARCENT, Combined Arms Assessment Team, Operation ENDURING FREEDOM (U), September 2002, p. vii, TFELR. (Secret//X1, X4).

[38] 20 ASOS/CC, "Interview with TFEL (U)," 19 August 2002. (Secret//X1, X4).

[39] 20 ASOS/CC, "Interview with TFEL (U)," 19 August 2002. (Secret//X1, X4).

[40] LTC U.S. Army, 10th Mountain Division, Fire Support Coordination Officer, "Interview with TFEL (U)," 30 Oct 2002. (Secret//X1, X4).

[41] General Myers, Interview with Wolf Blitzer, CNN, 10 March 2002.

[42] U.S. CENTCOM Process Review Panel Report for Fire Support Operations in Afghanistan (U), June 2002. (Secret//X1, X4).

[43] Point Paper, Operation Anaconda CFLCC Perspective (U), 16 March 2002. (Secret//X1, X4).

[44] Lt Gen Moseley, "Interview with TFEL (U)," 25 June 2003.

[45] COMCJTF Mountain OPORD 02-001, 231630Z FEB 2002, (U). (Secret//X1, X4).

[46] 20ASOS Maj, USAF, ALO in ASOC, "Interview with TFEL (U)," 20 May 2002. (Secret//X1, X4).

[47] 16 Feb 2002 air support cited in "Chronology of United States Central Command Air Forces (Forward) for Operation ENDURING FREEDOM, 1-28 Feb 2002. (U)." Entries for 16 Feb 2002 and 17 Feb 2002. (Secret//X1, X4).

[48] Briefing, USCENTCOM/J2 (U), 28 Feb 2002, TFELR. (Secret//X1, X4).

[49] Point Paper, Operation ANACONDA, CFLCC Perspective (U), 16 March 2002, (Secret//X1, X4).

[50] Lt Gen. Moseley, "Interview with TFEL (U)," 25 June 2003.

[51] Lt Gen. Moseley, "Interview with TFEL (U)," 25 June 2003.

[52] Lt Gen. Moseley, "Interview with TFEL (U)," 25 June 2003.

[53] Vernon Loeb, "General Defends Tactics in Afghan Battle," *Washington Post*, March 12, 2003.

[54] This interview 20 ASOS/CC discussion of TF *Dagger*'s initial plan. See, 20 ASOS Maj, "Interview with TFEL (U)," 20 May 2002. (Secret//X1, X4).

[55] Anaconda CONOPS Briefing, (U) 20 Feb 2002. (Secret//X1, X4).

[56] Anaconda CONOPS Briefing, (U) 20 Feb 2002. (Secret//X1, X4).

[57] Anaconda CONOPS Briefing, (U) 20 Feb 2002. (Secret//X1, X4).

[58] Anaconda CONOPS Briefing, (U) 20 Feb 2002. (Secret//X1, X4).

[59] Anaconda CONOPS Briefing, (U) 20 Feb 2002. (Secret//X1, X4).

[60] See also CJTF Mountain, "Operation ANACONDA Update Brief," (U) prepared 17 February 2002.

[61] Gen Moseley, "TFEL Interview (U)," 14 January 2003, TFELR. (Secret//X1, X4).

[62] COMCJTF Afghanistan Message, 201930ZFEB02, "COMCJTF Afghanistan Operations Order 02-001 (U)," 231630 February 2002, TFELR. (Secret//X1, X4).

[63] Report, CJTF *Mountain* to CFLCC (U), 162100Z Mar 2002. (Secret//X1, X4).

[64] Point Paper, Operation ANACONDA, CFLCC Perspective (U), 16 March 2002. (Secret//X1, X4).

[65] Point Paper, Operation ANACONDA, CFLCC Perspective (U), 16 March 2002. (Secret//X1, X4).

[66] Maj Gen John D. W. Corley, "Interview with TFEL (U)," 1 May 2002. (Secret//X1, X4).

[67] Maj Gen John D. W. Corley, USAF, "Interview with TFEL (U)," 3 January 2003. (Secret//X1, X4).

[68] Gen Moseley, "TFEL Interview (U)," 14 January 2003, TFELR. (Secret//X1, X4).

[69] This document cites AFCENT/HO Briefing notes, CFACC Missums, and Briefing Slides Files 16-18, 20-24. Chronology of United States Central Command Air Forces (Forward) for Operation ENDURING FREEDOM (U), 1-28 Feb 2002. (Secret//X1, X4).

[70] Chronology of United States Central Command Air Forces (Forward) for Operation ENDURING FREEDOM (U), 1-28 Feb 2002. (Secret//X1, X4).

[71] Maj Gen Corley, "Interview with TFEL (U)," 3 January 2003. (Secret//X1, X4).

[72] Lt Gen. Moseley, "Interview with TFEL (U)," 25 June 2003.

[73] HAF/XOE, Former CAOC Chief of Combat Ops, "Interview with TFEL (U)," 7 August 2002. (Secret//X1, X4).

[74] Commander, 18th Air Support Operations Group, "Interview with TFEL (U)," 9 May 2002. (Secret//X1, X4).

[75] ASOC Officer, Lt Col, USAF, with TF *K-Bar*, "Interview with TFEL (U)," 29 May 2002. (Secret//X1, X4).

[76] HAF/XOE, Former CAOC Chief of Combat Ops,, "Interview with TFEL (U)," 7 August 2002. (Secret//X1, X4).

[77] TFEL Interview with Lt Gen Moseley, (U) June 25, 2003.

[78] Major, USAF, USAF, "ASOC paper (U)," n.d., TFELR. (Secret//X1, X4).

[79] Lt Col, 682ASOS/CC, USAF, Commander of 682nd Air Support Operations Squadron, "Interview with TFEL (U)," 20 May 2002. (Secret//X1, X4).

[80] Lt Col 682ASOS/CC, " Interview with TFEL (U)," 20 May 2002. (Secret//X1, X4).

[81] 18 ASOG/CC, "Interview with TFEL (U)," 9 May 2002. (Secret//X1, X4).

[82] This assessment of uneven levels is from 20ASOS/CC and 682ASOS/CC, both discussing the issue. The quotes are 20ASOS/CC, for "very experienced SOF TACPs," and 682ASOS/CC for "wanted nothing to do with the conventional Air Force." See Lt Col 682ASOS/CC, "Interview with TFEL (U)," 20 May 2002. (Secret//X1, X4).

[83] This assessment of uneven levels is from 20ASOS/CC and 682ASOS/CC, both discussing the issue. The quotes are 20ASOS/CC, for "very experienced SOF TACPs," and 682ASOS/CC for "wanted nothing to do with the conventional Air Force." See Lt Col 682ASOS/CC, "Interview with TFEL (U)," 20 May 2002. (Secret//X1, X4).

[84] Lt Gen. Moseley, "Interview with TFEL (U)," 25 June 2003.

[85] 20ASOS/CC and 682ASOS/CC observations in TFEL Interview. Lt Col 682ASOS/CC "Interview with TFEL (U)," 20 May 2002. (Secret//X1, X4).

[86] ASOC Officer, Lt Col, USAF, "Interview with TFEL (U)," 29 May 2002. (Secret//X1, X4).

[87] Lt Gen Moseley, "Interview with TFEL (U)," 25 June 2003.

[88] Lt Gen Moseley, "Interview with TFEL (U)," 25 June 2003.

[89] The phrase, "Short of the FSCL," quoted in Point Paper, Operation ANACONDA, CFLCC Perspective (U), 16 March 2002. (Secret//X1, X4).

[90] Point Paper, Operation ANACONDA, CFLCC Perspective (U), 16 March 2002. (Secret//X1, X4).

[91] This comment made by Bochain in TFEL interview. Lt Col 682ASOS/CC, "Interview with TFEL (U)," 20 May 2002. (Secret//X1, X4).

[92] Lt Col 682ASOS/CC, "Interview with TFEL (U)," 20 May 2002. (Secret//X1, X4).

[93] Gen Moseley, "TFEL Interview (U)," 14 January 2003, TFELR. (Secret//X1, X4).

[94] 18ASOG/CC, "Interview with TFEL (U)," 9 May 2002. (Secret//X1, X4).

[95] Lt Col 682ASOS/CC, "Interview with TFEL (U)," 20 May 2002. (Secret//X1, X4).

[96] 20ASOS Maj, USAF, ALO in ASOC, "Interview with TFEL (U)," 20 May 2002. (Secret//X1, X4).

[97] Jim Fox, "West Point professors part of Afghan operation," Army News Services, May 9, 2002.

[98] Lt Col, USAF, "Interview with TFEL (U)." (Secret//X1, X4).

[99] 20ASOS Maj, USAF, ALO in ASOC, USAF, "Interview with TFEL (U)," 20 May 2002. (Secret//X1, X4).

[100] 20ASOS Maj, USAF, ALO in ASOC, "Interview with TFEL (U)," 20 May 2002. (Secret//X1, X4).

[101] Lt Col 682ASOS/CC, "Interview with TFEL (U)," 20 May 2002. (Secret//X1, X4).

[102] ASOC Officer, Lt Col, USAF, "Interview with TFEL (U)," 29 May 2002. (Secret//X1, X4).

[103] Lt Gen Moseley, "Interview with TFEL (U)," 25 June 2003.

[104] Gen Moseley, "TFEL Interview (U)," 14 January 2003, TFELR. (Secret//X1, X4).

[105] Maj Gen Corley, "Interview with TFEL (U)," 1 May 2002. (Secret//X1, X4).

[106] Gen Moseley, "TFEL Interview (U)," 14 January 2003, TFELR. (Secret//X1, X4).

[107] Robert H. McElroy, "Interview: Fire Support for Operation ANACONDA," *Field Artillery*, September-October 2002.

[108] Point Paper, Operation ANACONDA, CFLCC Perspective (U), 16 March 2002. (Secret//X1, X4).

[109] Gen Moseley, "TFEL Interview (U)," 14 January 2003, TFELR. (Secret//X1, X4).

[110] There is some confusion about who nominated the targets. General Moseley stated, "I was unable to get pre-strike targets." Generals Corley and Moseley stated in later interviews that they asked CFLCC to nominate targets, but the pre-strike targets were drawn from a list generated at PSAB. However, it appears that they were not made aware that CJTF *Mountain* had already compiled a list based on TF *11* information. Maj Gen Corley, "Interview with TFEL (U)," 3 January 2003. (Secret//X1, X4).

[111] Brig Gen Winfield Scott, USAF, Director of Mobility Forces in CAOC, "Interview with TFEL (U)," 11 February 2003. (Secret//X1, X4).

[112] Brig Gen Winfield Scott, USAF, Director of Mobility Forces in CAOC, "Interview with TFEL (U)," 11 February 2003. (Secret//X1, X4).

[113] Maj Gen Corley, "Interview with TFEL (U)," 1 May 2002. (Secret//X1, X4).

[114] Brig Gen Scott, "Interview with TFEL (U)," 11 February 2003. (Secret//X1, X4).

[115] 20ASOS Maj, USAF, ALO in ASOC, USAF, "Interview with TFEL (U)," 20 May 2002. (Secret//X1, X4).

[116] HQDA SITREP 169 (U), 010433Z Mar 2002. (Secret//X1, X4).

[117] Source is the MISREP for 2 Mar 2002 for Grim 33 and Grim 32 (U) located in TFELR collection. (Secret//X1, X4).

[118] This account from CENTCOM Chronology (U), June 2002. (Secret//X1, X4).

[119] HAF/XOE, CAOC Chief of Combat Ops, "Interview with TFEL (U)," 7 August 2002. (Secret//X1, X4).

[120] Gen Moseley, "TFEL Interview (U)," 14 January 2003, TFELR. (Secret//X1, X4).

[121] It was not discovered that the gunship had caused the incident until after Operation ANACONDA. General Franks said on 29 March 2002: "...as Operation Anaconda kicked off and the forces were moving into position, there was reporting of one of our convoys, a friendly convoy of American and Afghans, being under fire. Simultaneously, on a different radio network, I noticed reporting by an AC-130 gunship that it was engaging a convoy. I put the two things together and....so I've asked our Special Operations Component to investigate the facts…" DoD Press Conference with General Tommy Franks, Commander, US Central Command, Friday, March 29, 2002, official DoD Transcript.

[122] DoD Press Conference with General Tommy Franks, Commander, US Central Command, Friday, March 29, 2002, official DoD Transcript.

[123] After Action Report, 19th ASOS (U). (Secret//X1, X4).

[124] Message, CJTF MTN to CFLCC, "22100Z Mar 2002 (U)." (Secret//X1, X4).

[125] LTC Corkran quoted in Adam Geibel, "Operation ANACONDA, Shah-I-Kot Valley, Afghanistan, 2-10 March 2002," *Military Review* (Ft. Leavenworth, KS: May-June 2002.)

[126] Message, CFLCC SITREP (U), 021650Z March 2002. (Secret//X1, X4).

[127] Interview with U.S. Army Soldiers who Participated in Operation ANACONDA," March 7, 2002, Official DoD Transcript.

[128] Immediate CAS Database, DFSCOORD (U) data sheet. (Secret//X1, X4).

[129] 20ASOS Maj, USAF, ALO in ASOC, "Interview with TFEL (U)," 20 May 2002. (Secret//X1, X4).

[130] 20ASOS Maj, USAF, ALO in ASOC, "Interview with TFEL (U)," 20 May 2002. (Secret//X1, X4).

[131] Account of B-1 immediate CAS on 2 March 2002 is from MISREPs for Cyclone 01, Twister 01 and Tremor 01 (U). (Secret//X1, X4).

[132] Account of B-1 and AC-130 deconfliction is from MISREP for Blade 01, 2 March 2002 (U). (Secret//X1, X4).

[133] Message, CJTF MTN to CFLCC, "22100Z Mar 2002 (U)." (Secret//X1, X4).

[134] Marzak hostile—cited in CFLCC SITREP, 02 2200Z Mar 2002(U). (Secret//X1, X4).

[135] Maj Gen Corley, "Interview with TFEL (U)," 1 May 2002. (Secret//X1, X4).

[136] DoD News Briefing, Secretary Rumsfeld and General Franks, March 6, 2002, DoD Official Transcript.

[137] Message, CJTF MTN to CFLCC, "22100Z Mar 2002 (U)." (Secret//X1, X4).

[138] Message, CJTF MTN to CFLCC, "22100Z Mar 2002 (U)." (Secret//X1, X4).

[139] AC-130 MISREP for Grim 31, 2 March 2002, 16 SOS, Msn 4121 (U). (Secret//X1, X4).

[140] Requests for more helicopters noted in JOC Turnover Briefing (U), 3 March 2002. Requests dated 030909Z Mar 2002 and 031246Z Mar 2002. (Secret//X1, X4).

[141] Robert H. McElroy, "Interview: Fire Support for Operation ANACONDA," *Field Artillery*, September-October 2002.

[142] This number is from ACC's analysis of CAS response. The number varied daily.

[143] Maj Gen Corley, "Interview with TFEL (U)," 14 January 2003. (Secret//X1, X4).

[144] HAF/XOE, Former CAOC Chief of Combat Ops,, "Interview with TFEL (U)," 7 August 2002. (Secret//X1, X4).

[145] 20ASOS Maj, USAF, ALO in ASOC, "Interview with TFEL (U)," 20 May 2002. (Secret//X1, X4).

[146] Message, CJTF MTN to CFLCC, "22100Z Mar 2002 (U)." (Secret//X1, X4).

[147] Point Paper, Operation ANACONDA, CFLCC Perspective (U), 16 March 2002. (Secret//X1, X4).

[148] MISREP for Skynyrd 41 (Secret//X1, X4).

[149] 20ASOS Maj, USAF, ALO in ASOC, "Interview with TFEL (U)," 20 May 2002. (Secret//X1, X4).

[150] 20ASOS Maj, USAF, ALO in ASOC, "Interview with TFEL (U)," 20 May 2002. (Secret//X1, X4).

[151] 20ASOS Maj, USAF, ALO in ASOC, "Interview with TFEL (U)," 20 May 2002. (Secret//X1, X4).

[152] Immediate CAS statistics are from XCAS Database, DFSCOORD (U) data sheet. (Secret//X1, X4).

[153] Summary of March 3 operations quoted in CJTF *Mountain* to CFLCC (U), 032100Z Mar 2002. (Secret//X1, X4).

[154] TF *Rakkasan* TACP After-Action Report, Operation ANACONDA (U). (Secret//X1, X4).

[155] March 3 activities cited in CFLCC SITREP for 3 March 2002 (U). (Secret//X1, X4).

[156] Message, CJTF *Mountain* to CFLCC (U), 032100Z Mar 2002. (Secret//X1, X4).

[157] Staff Sergeant Richard D. Schleckser, USAF, 19ASOS, After Action Report (U). (Secret//X1, X4).

[158] DoD Briefing, "Background briefing on the Report of the Battle of Takur Ghar," May 24, 2002, official DoD Transcript.

[159] DoD Briefing, "Background briefing on the Report of the Battle of Takur Ghar," May 24, 2002, official DoD Transcript.

[160] DoD Briefing, "Background briefing on the Report of the Battle of Takur Ghar," May 24, 2002, official DoD Transcript.

[161] DoD Briefing, "Background briefing on the Report of the Battle of Takur Ghar," May 24, 2002, official DoD Transcript.

[162] Chronology of United States Central Command Air Forces (Forward) for Operation ENDURING FREEDOM (U), 1-31 Mar 2002. (Secret//X1, X4).

[163] From USCENTCOM Chronology (U), June 2002. (Secret//X1, X4).

[164] DoD Briefing, "Background briefing on the Report of the Battle of Takur Ghar," May 24, 2002, official DoD Transcript.

[165] MISREP for Twister 51 (U). (Secret//X1, X4).

[166] MISREP for Cujo 51 (U). (Secret//X1, X4).

[167] March 4 mission is in Center for Naval Analyses database of Navy MISREPs (U). (Secret//X1, X4).

[168] Lt Col 682ASOS/CC, "Interview with TFEL (U)," 20 May 2002. (Secret//X1, X4).

[169] Lt Col 682ASOS/CC, "Interview with TFEL (U)," 20 May 2002. (Secret//X1, X4).

[170] DoD Briefing, "Background briefing on the Report of the Battle of Takur Ghar," May 24, 2002, official DoD Transcript.

[171] DoD Briefing, "Background briefing on the Report of the Battle of Takur Ghar," May 24, 2002, official DoD Transcript. See also Staff Sergeant, "CSA Awards Silver Stars for Anaconda Valor," Army News Services, January 22, 2003.

[172] Account of insertion is from USCENTCOM Chronology (U). Numbers of personnel are from CJTF *Mountain* to CFLCC (S), 042100Z Mar 2002. (Secret//X1, X4).

[173] Lt Gen Moseley, "Interview with TFEL (U)," 25 June 2003.

[174] Additional source for this note is Memorandum from CENTAF Forward J3 (U), 4 Mar 2002. This is in the Army-Air Force Warfighter Talks smart book. (Secret//X1, X4).

[175] Lt Gen Moseley, "Interview with TFEL (U)," 25 June 2003.

[176] Lt Gen Moseley, "Interview with TFEL (U)," 25 June 2003.

[177] Senior Airman, USAF, GFAC call sign White Lightning Bravo, After-Action Report (U). (Secret//X1, X4).

[178] Captain, USAF, 74AEG/DOW, "Interview with Maj (U)," 6 May 2002. (Secret//X1, X4).

[179] Captain USAF, "Interview with Maj (U)," 6 May 2002. (Secret//X1, X4).

[180] CJTF *Mountain* to CFLCC (U), 042100Z Mar 2002. (Secret//X1, X4).

[181] Enemy casualty numbers cited in ANACONDA Daily SITREPs (U), (Secret//X1, X4).

[182] CJTF *Mountain* to CFLCC (U), 042100Z Mar 2002. (Secret//X1, X4).

[183] Gen Moseley, "TFEL Interview (U)," 14 January 2003, TFELR. (Secret//X1, X4).

[184] USCENTCOM Process Review Panel Report for Fire Support Operations in Afghanistan (U), June 2002. (Secret//X1, X4).

[185] Gen Moseley, "TFEL Interview (U)," 14 January 2003, TFELR. (Secret//X1, X4).

[186] 18ASOG/CC, "Interview with TFEL (U)," 9 May 2002. (Secret//X1, X4).

[187] Maj Gen Corley, "Interview with TFEL (U)," 3 January 2003. (Secret//X1, X4).

[188] Message, CJTF *Mountain* to CFLCC (U), 042100Z Mar 2002. (Secret//X1, X4).

[189] Message, CJTF *Mountain* to CFLCC (U), 052100Z Mar 2002. (Secret//X1, X4).

[190] USCENTCOM Process Review Panel Report for Fire Support Operations in Afghanistan (U), June 2002. (Secret//X1, X4).

[191] SITREP and JOC Turnover brief (U), 5 Mar 2002. (Secret//X1, X4).

[192] Brig Gen Scott, "Interview with TFEL (U)," 11 February 2003. (Secret//X1, X4).

[193] TF *Dagger* and TF *64* information including quotes and ordnance expended is from CJTF *Mountain* to CFLCC (U), 042100Z Mar 2002. (Secret//X1, X4).

[194] Message, CJTF *Mountain* to CFLCC (U), 052100Z Mar 2002. (Secret//X1, X4).

[195] Message, CJTF *Mountain* to CFLCC (U), 052100Z Mar 2002. (Secret//X1, X4).

[196] Captain, "Interview with Maj (U)," 6 May 2002. (Secret//X1, X4).

[197] See Center for Naval Analyses database for F/A-18s MISREPs (U). (Secret//X1, X4).

[198] Captain USAF, "Interview with Maj (U)," 6 May 2002. (Secret//X1, X4).

[199] Six A-10s attacked the al-Qaeda formation. Account of the A-10 attacks is in the MISREPs for Cherry 7, Cherry 3 and Cherry 1 for 5 March 2002 (U). (Secret//X1, X4).

[200] GFAC, Operation ANACONDA After Action Report (U), 15 March 2002. (Secret//X1, X4).

[201] Six A-10s attacked the al-Qaeda formation. Account of the A-10 attacks is in the MISREPs for Cherry 7, Cherry 3 and Cherry 1 for 5 March 2002 (U). (Secret//X1, X4).

[202] Quoted in CJTF *Mountain* to CFLCC (U), 062100Z Mar 2002. (Secret//X1, X4).

[203] See MISREP for Jazz *11* (U), 6 March 2002. (Secret//X1, X4).

[204] GFAC, USAF, 19ASOS, After Action Report, 19thASOS (U). (Secret//X1, X4).

[205] Gen Moseley, "TFEL Interview (U)," 14 January 2003, TFELR. (Secret//X1, X4).

[206] Gen Moseley, "TFEL Interview (U)," 14 January 2003, TFELR. (Secret//X1, X4).

[207] Commander of 332nd Expeditionary Operations Support Squadron, "Interview with Major, TFEL (U)," 4 June 2002. (Secret//X1, X4).

[208] U.S. Air Force, USCENTAF (Fwd) Collection Management, staff paper, "Tailoring ISR Products (U)," 17 April 2002, (Secret/X1,X4).

[209] 20ASOS Maj, USAF, ALO in ASOC, "Interview with TFEL (U)," 20 May 2002. (Secret//X1, X4).

[210] HAF/XOE, Former CAOC Chief of Combat Ops,, "Interview with TFEL (U)," 7 August 2002. (Secret//X1, X4).

[211] Gen Moseley, "TFEL Interview (U)," 14 January 2003, TFELR. (Secret//X1, X4).

[212] The phrase, *to bingo out*, has reached the fuel state calculated to return safely to the place of intended landing

[213] See MISREP for AC-130 Grim 31 (U). 7 March 2002 (Secret//X1, X4).

[214] Message, CJTF *Mountain* to CFLCC (U), 072100Z Mar 2002. (Secret//X1, X4).

[215] Message, CJTF *Mountain* to CFLCC (U), 072100Z Mar 2002. (Secret//X1, X4).

[216] Message, CJTF *Mountain* to CFLCC (U), 072100Z Mar 2002. (Secret//X1, X4).

[217] General Myers quoted in Interview with Wolf Blitzer, CNN, 10 March 2002.

[218] See AC-130 Grim 31 MISREP for 8 March 2002 (U). (Secret//X1, X4).

[219] Message, CFLCC SITREP 08 Mar 2002 (U). (Secret//X1, X4).

[220] MISREP for Braveheart 41, 8 March 2002, Mission ID 1205/XCAS (U). (Secret//X1, X4).

[221] Capt USAF, "Interview with Maj (U)," 6 May 2002. See also, Strike data from DFSCOORD database (S) (72200Z March 2002) (Secret//X1, X4).

[222] Account of Objective *Ginger* seizure compiled from CFLCC Daily SITREPS for 7-10 March 2002 (U). (Secret//X1, X4).

[223] Account of operations from CFLCC Daily SITREPS for 8-14 March 2002. Afghan commander force level from USCENTCOM Chronology (U), June 2002. (Secret//X1, X4).

[224] Mission report for Navy mission Lonewolf 11-14, Mission 1211, 11 March 2002 (U). (Secret//X1, X4).

[225] 13thMEU ACE ANACONDA Quick Look (U). (Secret//X1, X4).

[226] CJTF *Mountain* to CFLCC (U), 16 March 2002. (Secret//X1, X4).

[227] Canadian operations from CFLCC Daily SITREP logs, 10-16 March 2002 (U). (Secret//X1, X4).

[228] CJTF *Mountain* to CFLCC (U), 16 March 2002. (Secret//X1, X4).

[229] CJTF *Mountain* to CFLCC (U), 16 March 2002. (Secret//X1, X4).

[230] General Myers, "Interview with Wolf Blitzer, CNN," 10 March 2002.

[231] CJTF *Mountain* to CFLCC (U), 062100Z Mar 2002. (Secret//X1, X4).

[232] Gen Moseley, "TFEL Interview (U)," 14 January 2003, TFELR. (Secret//X1, X4).

[233] Maj Gen Corley, "Interview with TFEL (U)," 1 May 2002. (Secret//X1, X4).

[234] General Franklin L. Hagenbeck, U.S. Army, Commanding General of 10thMountain Division, in "Interview: Fire Support for Operation ANACONDA," *Field Artillery*, September-October 2002.

[235] Air Combat Command, Ninth Air Force, "CAS Responsiveness for ANACONDA," n.d., (Secret//X1, X4).

[236] USCENTCOM Process Review Panel Report for Fire Support Operations in Afghanistan (U), June 2002. (Secret//X1, X4).

[237] Message, CJTF *Mountain* to CFLCC (U), 16 March 2002. (Secret//X1, X4).

[238] DoD Press Conference, Secretary of Defense Rumsfeld and VCJCS General Peter Pace, March 15, 2002, official DoD transcript.

[239] Lt Col 682ASOS/CC, "Interview with TFEL (U)," 20 May 2002. (Secret//X1, X4).

[240] It was not discovered that the gunship had caused the incident until after Operation ANACONDA. General Franks said on 29 March 2002: "…as Operation Anaconda kicked off and the forces were moving

into position, there was reporting of one of our convoys, a friendly convoy of American and Afghans, being under fire. Simultaneously, on a different radio network, I noticed reporting by an AC-130 gunship that it was engaging a convoy. I put the two things together and….so I've asked our Special Operations Component to investigate the facts…" DoD Press Conference with General Tommy Franks, Commander, US Central Command, Friday, March 29, 2002, official DoD Transcript.

[241] Friendly casualty data is from 15 March 2002 ARCENT Daily SITREP (U). (Secret//X1, X4).

[242] Revised enemy strength data is from 15 March 2002 ARCENT Daily SITREP (U). (Secret//X1, X4).

[243] Enemy casualty from 15 March 2002 ARCENT Daily SITREP (U). (Secret//X1, X4).

[244] Maj Gen Corley, "Interview with TFEL (U)," 2 January 2003. (Secret//X1, X4).

[245] CFLCC manning is reported in ARCENT, Combined Arms Assessment Team (CAAT), Operation ENDURING FREEDOM (September 2002) (U), p. 45.

[246] Gen Moseley, "TFEL Interview (U)," 14 January 2003, TFELR. (Secret//X1, X4).

[247] Lt Gen. Moseley, "Interview with TFEL (U)," 25 June 2003.

[248] Point Paper, Operation ANACONDA, CFLCC Perspective (U), March 16, 2002. (Secret//X1, X4).

[249] Gen Moseley, "TFEL Interview (U)," 14 January 2003, TFELR. (Secret//X1, X4).

[250] 20ASOS Maj, USAF, ALO in ASOC, "Interview with TFEL (U)," 20 May 2002. (Secret//X1, X4).

[251] Gen Moseley, "TFEL Interview (U)," 14 January 2003, TFELR. (Secret//X1, X4).

[252] Lt Gen Moseley, "Interview with TFEL (U)," 25 June 2003.

[253] General Franks, "DoD Special Briefing on Takur Gar (U)," 31 May 2002. (Secret//X1, X4).

[254] Gen Moseley, "TFEL Interview (U)," 14 January 2003, TFELR. (Secret//X1, X4).

[255] Lt Gen Moseley, "Interview with TFEL (U)," 25 June 2003.

[256] GFAC, Combat Controller Technician, Kandahar, Afghanistan, "Interview with Major USAF, TFEL (U)." n.d. (Secret//X1, X4).

www.ingramcontent.com/pod-product-compliance
Lightning Source LLC
Chambersburg PA
CBHW080515110426
42742CB00017B/3128